T0208537

# PERSONAL FINANCE:
## YOUR ROADMAP TOWARDS CREATING WEALTH AND FINANCIAL LITERACY

*(Basic guide to earning, saving, money management and investing)*

KENETH DALE R. TUAZON

**author**HOUSE®

*AuthorHouse™*
*1663 Liberty Drive*
*Bloomington, IN 47403*
*www.authorhouse.com*
*Phone: 833-262-8899*

*Published by AuthorHouse  11/19/2021*

*ISBN: 978-1-6655-4398-9 (sc)*
*ISBN: 978-1-6655-4397-2 (hc)*
*ISBN: 978-1-6655-4538-9 (e)*

*Library of Congress Control Number: 2021923182*

# Contents

Expectations.................................................................vii
Introduction ................................................................ix


## Part 1:  The Basics will Keep You on the Right Track

**Chapter 1:  All About Financial Literacy**.............................. 1
    Your Money Foundation ................................................ 2
    Your Journey Towards Financial Success ...................... 5
**Chapter 2:  Nurturing Your Financial Health**........................ 12
    Identifying All Your Money Mistakes............................ 12
    Determining Your Financial Net Worth ....................... 20
    Examining Your Credit Score and Reports .................. 24
    Bad Debt Versus Good Debt ...................................... 26
**Chapter 3:  Creating and Reaching Goals**............................ 33
    Articulate the Right Definition of Wealth.................... 34
    Your Saving Goals Inventory ...................................... 36
    Save to Buy a House or Business ............................... 38
**Chapter 4:  Money Come and Go**...................................... 40
    Examining Overspending ........................................... 41
    Scrutinizing Your Spending........................................ 44


## Part 2:  Spending Less, Saving More

**Chapter 5:  Using Credit and Debt Prudently** ..................... 51
    Use Savings to Cut Your Consumer Debt ................... 51
    Using the Debt Cycle Wisely ..................................... 52
**Chapter 6:  Reducing Your Spending** ................................. 54
    Revealing the Keys to Responsible Spending............. 54
    Boost Your Savings through Budgeting ..................... 59

## Part 3: Building Wealth through Investing

**Chapter 7: Invest Your Time and Money Wisely**.................................. **69**

    Build Your Goals................................................................ 69

    Anticipate Investment Risks .......................................... 71

    Investments Diversification .......................................... 76

    The New Path of Investment Probabilities ................. 86

    Discovering Various Types of Fund.............................. 97

**Chapter 8: Insurance: Protect What You Have** ................... **108**

    The Three Rules of Buying Insurance ......................... 109

    Protect Your Loved Ones: Life Insurance................... 115

**Chapter 9: Blueprint for Financial Success** ........................ **117**

    Getting Started ............................................................... 118

    Finding for Your Passion/Career .................................. 119

    Settling for Marriage ..................................................... 120

    Having a Home................................................................ 120

    Having Children............................................................... 121

    Opening a Small Business.............................................. 122

    Retiring............................................................................. 123


Book References ...................................................................... 125

Tips for Financial Success....................................................... 127

Author's Acknowledgement ................................................... 131

About the Author ..................................................................... 133

# *Expectations*

I have some expectations about you, dear reader:

- You want a piece of qualified advice about critical financial topics (such as saving, paying off, and reducing your cost of debt, planning for your primary goals, and making wise investments). And you want a speedy response.
- You want a basic guide in personal finance. You are looking for a comprehensive book you can read to solidify your financial conceptions and help you think about your finances more systematically.

This book is basic enough to help everyone get their arms around curvy financial issues. But it challenges advanced readers to think about their finances in a new way and identify areas for improvement.

# *Introduction*

Talking about money and finance has been one of the underrated topics. Maybe because a lot of us were not oriented on such. Most of us are not personal finance experts, for a good reason. All we know is that, you work to have a wage or salary and do business to earn money.

Most of the people who got some financial education and are acquainted with financial knowledge thru the years are likely to be busy people struggling with managing time. Speaking of time management, no one can manage time the way it used to be. Time is running, and you cannot control it. All you can do is discipline yourself and your activities. Managing your activities is better than pressuring yourself to hold your time. Most of us wish to know how to diagnose our financial status to know what to do. Some may have found out the problem. The thing is, choosing the suitable alternative is overwhelming. There are several types of investments, insurance, and loan options to choose from. The internet is full of information, but the hard part is choosing the best one.

I have tried different investment options in the past. Nothing succeeded until I found out that a proper mindset will bring me to my goals. Even if one has huge capital or great strategies in doing business, it will be useless if his/her perspectives don't align with the goals.

The problem with investing in this generation is that, people go with what they are hyped for. You may have heard about financial products through online ads that can be misleading and which promise you wealth in a get rich-easy scheme that is so good to be true. Getting rich-quick is possible if you work smart, but getting rich-easy is a big scam.

Because of false advertisements, the internet made wealth easy to find. Thus, making people commit the same financial mistake repeatedly—no goals, procrastinating, unnecessary spending, absence of planning, and failing to do serious research before making sound financial decisions. This guide can keep you away from the same common mistakes and embrace your true wealth, YOU!

You may say that the world is unfair because some are blessed, and you are not. But, unfortunately, the world is shaky, and the only way to at least ride with it is to keep the positivity and know the financial basics.

There are lots of one-sided and wrong financial advices; while some made me broke. I used to get and listen to the consequences of poor suggestions. Money is not an end in itself but a part of our whole life, whether we like it or not.

This book helps you understand your financial goals and solve challenges that may come your way. We all need is a deeper understanding of personal finance that includes all parts of your financial lifecycle: saving and investing, spending, someday running your own business or company, and the like.

Understanding the financial basics could be challenging which makes it difficult to think about your finances holistically. However, the reality is, our financial decisions reflect the history of our life, our parents, and the status quo more than they reflect our future.

# Part 1
## The Basics will Keep You on the Right Track

What is your current personal financial health?

What is your financial blueprint?

How can you accomplish your financial goals?

# Chapter 1
# All About Financial Literacy

---

*For every effect, there is a root cause. Find and address the root cause*
*rather than try to fix the effect, as there is no end to the latter.*
*- Celestine Chua, Founder, Personal Excellence Blog*

---

Financial literacy is a thing most people don't want to talk about. Aside from the notion that it all pertains to money, most people don't want to admit their financial mistakes.

In my years of work experience, from being a financial data analyst, sales associate, business consultant to business and finance teacher, I found out that many people indeed have significant gaps in their personal financial knowledge. However, most of us through the internet have greater access to more information than in the past generations. The growing financial world, compared to the past with limited access to information has become so complicated. Vast of choices has opened but is prone to financial dangers.

Unfortunately, most people are not aware of managing their personal finances because no one has ever taught them how to do so. Parents have avoided discussing financial matters, most especially money with them. Although colleges and universities offer financial courses nowadays, most students and teachers lack proper applications that instill this vital, lifetime-needed skill.

Some people are blessed-enough to acquire the secrets to financial success at home. Personally, our parents didn't have the means to learn all the technicalities about personal finance from their roots, that's why they didn't have something to teach us. Speaking of money matters, they were conservative yet generous to us. In terms of diligence and hard work, they are incomparable. They did everything just to make ends meet and provide for us.

I experienced many financial challenges because I never discovered crucial personal finance concepts. I learned most of them the hard way — by making many costly mistakes. However, it did not stop me from there, so I continued studying Personal Finance. Those who lack information make more mistakes, and the more financial faults they commit, the more money they lose. If you experience a massive financial loss, you will be emotionally disturbed of not feeling in control of your finances. Countless emotional stress and anxiety go hand in hand if you cannot overcome and control them.

You'll soon realize where individuals learn about their finances. How it may help one resolve his financial problem depends on the current level of information that holds him back. Taking responsibility for your finances will help you improve your financial literacy. It keeps you in charge and reduce your burdens about money.

## Your Money Foundation

As I was growing up, my parents showed me many things that have been helpful throughout my life. Some of these were basic principles for farming, selling, wise spending, and saving. They had to know how to do these things because they were raising four children while relying on agriculture as their source of income. Therefore, they valued every cent of the peso and understood the importance of making the most of what they had and it was a credit of passing that vital skill on to us, their children.

My parents had also been financially challenged. Catastrophic events hit their crops, my grandfather was diagnosed with cancer, and some farmlands had to be sold. We knew we had to work hard because life is hard. We needed to accompany them and sell vegetables for us to have school allowances after weekends. My parents' financial knowledge was not technically perfect. I saw them struggle financially. This situation has driven me to learn about investing to help myself, my family, and others.

*For some parents, money is off-limits because they don't want to talk with their children about their budget's boundaries, realities, and details. When asked why they don't involve their children, some parents believe that dealing with money is a grown-up issue. And that children have to be excluded from the responsibility just to enjoy childhood. Others freely disclose the loopholes in their financial knowledge, so they don't feel comfortable teaching their children about money. The hard part is that, children hear about money only when parents have disagreements and disputes for financial difficulties. In these cases, children begin to have negative notions and associations with money and financial management.*

On the other hand, some parents, even with good intentions, transfer their bad money-management habits to their children. For example, your parent may have told you to buy things to cheer yourself up when you're lonely. You may have seen a family member chasing get-rich-quick scheme and investment ideas. That is not supposed to be the problem. Your parents are right at some point, but poor financial advice and molding can be a significant problem in your financial future.

Digging up, look at where your parents learned about money management, and then reflect whether they had the time and energy to search for options before making financial decisions. For example, supposedly, there has never been enough financial information; your parents may incorrectly think saving in banks was like investing money, and, investing in stocks and currencies was like gambling and giving It away.

In some cases, where parents have the right financial approach, but the children misinterpret such. For example, suppose your parents are careful and strict about spending, and sometimes you feel denied. In that case, when money comes your way, you buy a lot of stuff and endless gifts for yourself; it may not be harmful, but you'll end up overspending.

Our educational system is overwhelming; we can't change what our parents did or didn't teach us about money management. So all we can do is to find out what we need to know to manage our finances.

*If you have kids, don't misjudge them and their potentials, or worst, don't let them grow with the thinking that money is just a thing that you can just take for granted. Remember that money will treat you the way you treat it. To be wise and productive about money, advise them to read financial books prior and as they start college and into their job.*

## Personal Finance Education

During my college time, Personal Finance was never taught and not readily available. There was no ready book, no internet or google, and no access to any financial information.

The problem with personal finance education is that, it is not infused in elementary school. In addition, some may argue that the subject matter is too complex for children to understand. Still, the point is, it should be used as an application to significant subjects like Mathematics, Home economics, and other related courses.

Fundamental concepts were taught in the elementary grade. If personal finance were incorporated into math classes to illustrate how math can be used in the real world, students would be prepared as they grow. Nowadays, there are available virtual games relating to Personal Finance that are interactive. For example, Students may choose a career, find jobs, and figure out their take-home pay. The teacher shall guide them. They then have to decide how they spend their money. They will be given spending choices to guide them in budgeting and spending their Income. They may also Invest "play money" in a particular investment vehicle which the teacher identified and then acts as the regulator. The rate of returns per investment vehicle in a given period shall be given to the students, and then they will choose which to invest in. Investment options will also be available to them. The teacher then monitors how the students earned, spent, and invested their money at the end of the term. Finally, the teacher awards students who accomplished the tasks well.

Asking schools to impart the fundamentals of personal finance is just mutual wisdom. Children must be educated on managing a daily budget, the importance of saving money for future goals, and the downsides of overspending. Sadly, only a few schools teach the concepts of Personal Finance.[1] And worst, the financial basics aren't taught at all.

Though some schools offer courses closely related to Personal Finance, like economics, the application is much broader. Fundamental theories being taught doesn't do anything for the students as far as preparing them for the real world is concerned. When I was in college, the subject was so broad that it was too much to absorb. I just appreciated the value of the course when I was already using it and into my business.

We may say that parents must teach their children the basics of financial management. Still, this sentiment is what the future generation is relying upon. Unfortunately, for some, it is not working because a lot of parents are hesitant. Worst-case scenario, financial illiteracy is passed on to succeeding generations.

Education shall start at home, but it is more emphasized in the schools. Hence, schools have to take responsibility for teaching essential skills. Whether you teach your children about personal finance at home, the problem keeps coming back to you. Besides, no one cares about the welfare of your family as much as you do. Children quickly immitate and may duplicate what they actually see at home. Therefore, proper and responsible money management should start in you.

## Your Journey Towards Financial Success

Maybe you are aware of this adage: *live within your means, have suitable long-term investments, and secure proper insurance coverage.* So easy to say, but in reality, it may not be as easy as it seems to be. Living below or within your means may not always be helpful. You must upgrade your learning day to day, create multiple income streams, and have a steady cash flow.

Breaking the bad habits will always be the biggest challenge you encounter along the way. Series of temptations like spending

---

[1] https://businessmirror.com.ph/2019/08/12/deped-bsp-push-financial-literacy-lessons-to-students/

impulsively keeps coming in. Ads and promotions ring you every time there are sales or discounts. Social media fascinates you about people enjoying luxurious travel, expensive cars, and mansions. You felt deprived because your parents were tight regarding money or maybe you were bored, so that buying new things satisfy you. You also want to hit big on your investments, get rich, and do all the things you want to do with your life.

These can only be achievable if we think and feel the right way. However, everything is possible because the mind is limitless. Don't let emotions and temptations control you. You prevent them, instead. Undoubtedly, the portion of effectively managing your finances includes admitting your shortcomings and the consequences of your behaviors. After admission, correct them immediately. If you don't, you may end up trapped in dead-end employment so you can keep nursing your spending obsessions. Or you may just keep on working on your business or investments without any leverage other than spending time with your family.

## Discovering the Roots of your Financial Problems

Many personal and emotional obstacles can get in the way of making the best financial moves. Like what has been discussed earlier, lack of financial knowledge may affect making sound financial decisions.

I've known some people locked in the psychological trap of blaming someone or something else for their financial problems. For example, some people believe that grown-up issues can be mapped back from childhood. The problem most people do is that they blame their parents, the government, their situation for their lack of financial planning. They jumped out on the thinking – if only. For example, some people say: If only I were rich or If only my family were rich. They also say, If only my salary is high, If only the government is not corrupt, or If only there is no crisis, and etc. These kinds of mentality may not solve the problem. It may just worsen because what you focus is on expands. Always focus on the good side and be accountable for your actions. Learn to correct your mistakes and move on.

In the book of T. Harv Eker, *Secrets of the Millionaire Mind*, our money mindset is essential. We acquired most of them from our parents and the people around us.[2] The way we see money entails our financial standing. And since we were programmed financially, we carry them as we grow. Even if you are smart and have the necessary skills to become wealthy, you will not achieve what you want if your mind is not aligned with them. The question is; *Can you still change that? How?* The answer is *yes*. The good thing to do is to admit and accept the roots of the problem and then shift your mind to erasing such past and replace them with a brand new, healthy financial mindset. Every day when you wake up and before going to sleep, always be positive and be grateful. You just need to reversely program the negatively taught concepts to you about money like being unfortunate, being not worthy, being limited, money is evil, etc. *(They were listed in the next segment)*

> In reprogramming, have some positive affirmations about yourself every day of your life. Like, *I am Rich in all aspects of my life, I am worthy, I am Limitless*, etc. Say all the positive things you could ever think to your mind without any doubt. At first, your mind won't believe them, just push it. It may sound absurd, but yes, repetition will get you there. Like we all hear, in any field or aspect, good and correct practice makes perfect. Believe it.

As Bob Proctor said, *Always feed your mind with positive affirmations*. For example, *I am so happy and grateful now, that money comes to me in increasing quantities through multiple sources on a continuous basis.*[3] or *Money flows into my life with ease and abundance, Money flows out with gratitude and love.*

A lot of people blame their actions for not earning more income. They believed that more revenue would solve all their problems. My

---

[2] **T. Harv Eker**, author, professional speaker, businessman, and the founder of seminar company "Peak Potentials Training". He is also the author of "Speed Wealth" and "True Wealth" and other co-authored books.

[3] **Bob Proctor**, a self-help author and philosopher. He is best known for his New York Times best-selling book You Were Born Rich and a contributor to the film The Secret. His material has maintained the idea that a positive self-image is critical for obtaining success, frequently referencing the Law of Attraction. This includes all the books he has authored as well as seminars he conducted, and videos shared in Youtube.

experiences, so with others taught me that happiness does not depend on how much money you earn but on how you view life. I knew about financially-able and wealthy people who, depite of their abundance are still emotionally challenged. At the same time, I knew of people who were pretty happy and emotionally contented but financially challenged. Money is just a thing that will magnify your current life views. Personal happiness depends on personal opinions, not on the money that you have.

Your money blueprint and how you perceive money are the main reasons you are in your current financial state.

Personal Finance is much more than handling and investing money well. It also includes connecting all the dots of your financial life. It means getting yourself out of financial problems. Like any other planning process, managing your finances means creating a plan to wisely use your money and time.

Whoever you are and whatever your current financial state right now, your view about money and being wealthy will lead you to the abundance or maybe the opposite.

Culture, tradition, people we look-up-to, and even the people around us contribute a lot to our money mindset. Here are some wrong perceptions about money:

1. **Money is evil.** Connecting money with sin is the worst argument you can ever consider. Money doesn't determine your personality. It will just amplify it. Suppose you are a good person and you became wealthy. In that case, you think of ways to use your money in good purpose, like providing for your family and friends, helping the needy, and funding charities. If you are a bad person, you might spend your money in the wrong ways. People who believe that money is the root of all evil tend to stay away from it because they don't want to become evil. So the choice is actually dependent upon you, not on the money.

2. **Money is just a printed paper. It is not the most important thing in the world.** It may perhaps not be the most important thing, but you need money to survive some areas of your life. Your food, shelter, clothing, and your necessities, even your self-enhancement and improvement activities. If you consider money unimportant, you will not value it. If you appreciate it well, it will stay with you. If you misuse it, it will go away.

3. **Being wealthy is greedy.** Greed is not dependent on wealth. It is a self-driven personality. I knew of people who were rich yet selfless and generous. For example, Warren Buffet, a billionaire and a philanthropist, donated more than half of its net worth to charities.[4] I also knew of people who were poor and yet still were selfless and willing to sacrifice for others. Wealth is just a financial state that will amplify personalities. Being greedy is a choice. Choose generosity.

4. **Money is hard to earn.** Most people were programmed this way. Some parents transfer this mindset to their downline of generation. This mindset will shut down the different ideas on how to earn money. Saying *how can I?* is better than saying *I can't*. Suppose you always think that it is hard to make money, and in that case, you will look for ways to achieve it comfortably. Tendencies are that you will just trade your time for it. Don't get me wrong, what I'm saying is that the word should not be *hard* or *I can't*. It must be *possible* or *How can I?* In this case, your mind will be challenged to think about how you can earn money from multiple sources. If you think that money is hard to reach, you will quickly give up and struggle financially.

5. **You need to have a college degree or diploma before you can earn money.** Whether degree holder or not, you have the opportunity to make money. Your earning capacity doesn't depend on your educational attainment. I had known people who do not have any degree/s yet are financially successful

---

[4] **Warren Edward Buffett,** investor and businessman, the CEO and largest shareholder of Berkshire Hathaway, a multinational conglomerate holding. He is considered to be one of the richest people and most influential philanthropists of today. He wrote the book "My philanthropic pledge" published in 2010. Due to his charitable donations, he was awarded **Presidential Medal of Freedom** which is the highest civilian honor in the USA.

in life. It's not your diploma that will dictate you to earn money; it is your decision to act right away. It is just a matter of perseverance and working smart. Then, you can start earning money as early as you can. The right time will not come if you do not decide that it is the right time.

6. **Money can't buy you happiness and love.** The goal is not to buy love and happiness. Both of these are not dependent on money and wealth. You can have both love and joy even without money. But having money and wealth will emphasize your love for your family and others. It will also amplify your happiness and theirs.

7. **Be content with what you have.** This limiting belief will stop you from chasing your dreams. *Be grateful for what you have,* instead. Being grateful allows a more significant opportunity for success in all aspects of your life. Entrepreneur Jim Rohn said, *Learn to be thankful for what you already have while you pursue all that you want.*[5] Always choose growth over contentment. In that way, you can expand your ways to help yourself, your family, and friends and fulfill your true purpose in life.

8. **You cannot bring your wealth to the grave.** The premise is true, but you can leave it behind with your heirs. Most people think that they do not need wealth because everyone will die at some point. This kind of mindset kills dreams and possibilities. It means that you do not want to grow financially. It is a selfish motive. Building wealth means you are thinking of the welfare of the future generation.

Knowing the correct answers is insufficient. You have to apply them in your life. Forming a habit comes from repetition. Practicing a good mindset and financial habits will make you a step closer to your financial goals.

Don't be overwhelmed. Make a list of your financial marching orders and start working away. You have to overcome temptations and keep

---

[5] **Jim Rohn,** a renowned author, motivational speaker, entrepreneur and business coach. He is famous in the world for his influencing skills that mostly changed people's lives. He had authored over 20 books in his life including "The Art of Exceptional Living".

control of your money rather than let your emotions and money rule you.

Your money is your responsibility. It is a pretty personal and confidential matter. I hope you will be challenged to think about money and make sound personal financial decisions throughout your financial journey.

I also want to impart some wisdom about the meaning of life, nurturing the mind, and becoming productive. I may not be a philosopher, but I know that money is necessary and connected with some areas of our lives.

# Chapter 2
# Nurturing Your Financial Health

*If you are disciplined enough to succeed, you are*
*already one step closer to your dreams.*
*– K.D. Tuazon*

You now understand that your current situation was the effect of your decisions and your mindset. If you are rich, it is a manifestation that you aligned your abundant mindset towards success. On the other hand, if you're poor, you thought about the wrong perceptions about money and limited your beliefs. Make time to shift your mind from thinking you are *lacking* to *being abundant*.

Are you financially healthy? Do you review your overall financial situation? Are you tracking and analyzing your spending, savings, and future goals? Like your new year's resolution, you've got things to work on if you are not doing these things yet.

This segment guides you through a financial checkup to help you identify your current financial health problems. But don't focus on those problems. Instead, treat them as your basis for improvement.

In fact, being courageous in acknowledging those problems, the greater the potential you may have to solve them all and accomplish your financial and life goals.

## *Identifying All Your Money Mistakes*

Financial Problems like any other medical condition are best detected as early as possible. In this way, potential solutions to avoid or prevent them will be immediately taken into action. Prevention is better than cure. Here are the common financial mistakes most people make:

- **Lack of financial planning.** There's a statement, *If you fail to plan, you plan to fail.* Most people procrastinate. They think that *It's too early to plan.* Unlike any other institution like the government, you don't set an explicit deadline on your financial goals. Planning your finances may not be your primary priority, but doing so can help you get out of the financial dilemma.

- **Too much spending.** In simple Math, you know that your savings are the difference between what you earn and what you spend. So you may either increase your learning to earn more or preferably spend less than what you earn. Entrepreneur Robert Kiyosaki said that it's not how much money you make but how much money you keep.[6] Being thrifty or frugal is good, but you have to note many opportunities to earn money. The creation of multiple streams of income helps you increase your savings and build your financial foundation.

- **Being Lazy and full of excuses.** Most people don't go ahead in life because of laziness. Making excuses is the brother of laziness. All your reasons are correct, and they are the justifications for your laziness. The consequence is that, you will not make a move to improve your financial state. You don't want to work; you depend on your parents, friends, and others. You love to sleep, and the bed is your best friend. The bible says that poverty will come upon you like a robber if you love sleep and folding of the hands. Proverbs 20:4 stated that *The sluggard will not plow by reason of the cold; therefore, shall he beg in harvest, and have nothing.*[7]

- **Playing the blame game.** *Lame people blame people.* Take responsibility for your own life. Your current reality is because of you, your mindset, your attitude, and your decisions. In the book of Brother Bo Sanchez; he said, *Blame robs you of your*

---

[6] **Robert Kiyosaki**, a self-made businessman, investor, author and motivational speaker. He is the founder of the extremely well known and successful 'Rich Dad Poor Dad' brand, and the author of over 23 different books. He said that saving money should be a short-term proposition. You should only save money while looking for your next investment. When the right investment appears, invest the money you've been saving in something that will give you a higher rate of return.

[7] The Bible, (A) Proverbs 19:15 (NLT) Lazy people sleep soundly, but idleness leaves them hungry. (B) Proverbs 24:34 (NLT) Then poverty will pounce on you like a bandit; scarcity will attack you like an armed robber. (C) Proverbs 20:4 (NKJV) The lazy man will not plow because of winter; He will beg during harvest and have nothing.

*power to determine your life.*[8] If you do the blame game, you will not learn because you think you are right all the time. You will continue to make the wrong decisions in your life. Accept your mistakes and humbly change for the better.

- **More talks, less action.** *Action speaks louder than words.* Most people talk a lot. They share what they want to do, what they believe in, their plans, dreams, and goals, and so what? Talk is cheap. These are meaningless if you will not do the work. It's good to talk about your dreams, goals, and plans, but be sure to commit to getting them. When you commit, it means that you will do whatever it takes to achieve them, not just when it is convenient.

- **Lack of reading and lack of research.** Lack of research and reading materials are the two principal factors that prevent people from getting the best deal on financial success. Billionaire Investor Warren Buffet spends 5-6 hours of his day reading. Billionaire tech entrepreneur Elon Musk learned how to build rockets by reading books. Bill Gates, a billionaire philanthropist, is a lifelong bookworm who reads about 50 books a year. Similarly, Mark Zuckerberg, the founder of Facebook, invited the whole world to read a book every two weeks.[9] Remember that the world's most successful individuals have one thing in common – they value books and appreciate reading.

- **Deciding based on emotions.** You are more vulnerable to making the wrong financial decisions when feeling pressured or experiencing a significant life change. Or maybe, after losing a job, you just feel like giving up on life because of financial problems. There are times when you should start planning for, how you will feel once you have lost your job plus your what-ifs. Don't decide when you're too emotional. Instead, make time to think about how you feel. Financial Coach and Author Chinkee

---

[8] **Eugenio Isabelo Tomas Reyes Sanchez Jr.** a.k.a **Bother Bo Sanchez,** a Catholic lay preacher and minister, motivational speaker, a best-selling author and entrepreneur. He authored the book "8 Secrets of the Truly Rich" and founder of the "Truly Rich Club", a place where you can gain spiritual and financial abundance.

[9] (A) https://www.blinkist.com/magazine/posts/reading-habits-of-highly-successful-people
(B) https://www.thesouljam.com/post/the-powerful-habit-of-billionaires

Tan said, *money is not a number you think but an emotional thing.*[10] Letting money overpower you will lead to eternal financial problems. Don't let money control you; instead, you should be controlling it.

- **Lack of savings and investments.** Most people take these two for granted. They believe that saving money is just for those earning big, and investing is just for the rich. However, whether you are earning big or small, saving and investing will increase your net worth exponentially. These are the perfect combo in your financial journey.
- **Focusing too much on the material things.** For some, money is not always the first priority in people's lives. Focusing too much on money will make a person materialistic. You sacrifice losing some of what makes you feel human. You will forget that money is just a tool that will amplify the good in you. Choose the good side.
- **No dreams and goals.** Having no dream is like driving a car with no definite destination. Dreams and goals set our target. They fuel our potentials and give us a sense of motivation. Value your dreams and unleash your utmost potential. Remember that if you have a dream, you will know what you are willing to give up in order to go up.

Bad money habits can be fixed over time. But, first, recognize that it is a bad habit and that you are committed to changing it. Also, remember that a habit is both a good friend and a bad enemy.

## Structure Your Good Financial Habits

A habit is made through repetition. It is the result of our recurring actions. Philosopher Aristotle quoted, *We are what we repeatedly do. Excellence, then, is not an act but a habit.*

---

[10] **Chinkee Tan** a.k.a **"Mr. Chink Positive!"**, a financial expert, motivational speaker, radio and TV personality, entrepreneur and the author of "Till Debt Do Us Part: Practical Steps to Financial Freedom" and other best-selling books. He is passionate in helping people experience financial freedom and a debt-free living.

Bestselling author Steven Covey defines a habit as the *intersection of knowledge, skill, and desire.*[11] Knowledge implies the *what to do* and the *why*. Skill is the *how to do*. And the desire fuels the motivation, the *want to do*. Thus, to create a habit in our lives, the three should be unified as one.

It can be hard to start new habits, especially when it comes to breaking the bad ones. But, establishing a good habit can lead to long-term changes and a sense of satisfaction. Since we are the product of our actions, we have to commit to improving for the better.

Sometimes, it is painful to make a change. It's a process that pushes one to accept what one wants now, and it can be motivated by a higher purpose. The goal is to create priceless joy. A joyful life is defined as the object and design of our being. The process produces what the object of our existence is. It can be seen as the fruit of our desire to sacrifice everything for something bigger.

Learning how habits work helps people develop effective habits. Once they break, they can be easily controlled. Good habits are those that help you live your best life. While they are very important, some of them may seem a bit hard to follow, but thru discipline, they are achievable. Here are some rules to consider in developing your good financial habits.

- **Begin your day with meditation.** Mindful meditation helps place yourself at the moment. It makes you prepared for the various challenges that may arise during the day. For example, different stress levels can trigger different actions and behaviors, resulting in distractions and a lack of focus in all aspects. They also disturb your calmness. Having a good habit of meditation can help you manage these different factors.
- **Master the art of visualization.** Visualization is also a good habit to have. By visualizing a certain event or situation in your life,

---

[11] **Steven Covey,** an exceptional personality renowned for his work as a successful businessman, educator, and an influential public speaker. He is the author of one of the best-selling business books of the twentieth century, "The Seven Habits of Highly Effective People."

you can attract it into your mind. This natural occurrence is referred to as the power of thoughts.[12] It works by allowing yourself to visualize your goals and attract the success you desire in your life. The subconscious mind is a mental rehearsal when you repeat the thoughts and images that you often have in your mind. This rehearsal changes how you behave and react. Your thoughts and mental images can trigger new experiences and alter the way you see the world. They can also transform the way you interact with people. As part of the Omnipotent Power[13], we are part of the universe's creation process. This explains why the thoughts that come out of our mouths seem to materialize.

- **Always smile.** A happy and healthy life is a habit that can be maintained by smiling constantly. This is because it can trigger a variety of emotions and actions that are related to happiness. For instance, a smiling happy face can help people feel more confident and calm.

- **Be grateful.** Most people tend to waste time focusing on what's not enough. Instead of focusing on the things that are not enough, try focusing on what you have. Gratitude is an influential tool to shift our focus away from what we don't have towards what we have. It opens the possibilities of growth and development. By being grateful, we positively commit to achieving the things that we want. It can help you improve your health, happiness, and success. It can be done in various ways. You can begin by writing a list of the things that you are grateful for each day.

- **Exercise daily and eat healthily.** It is good to be physically active. It is also vital to have a good habit of doing at least 15-20 minutes of exercise each day. It could be a jogging, biking, stationary walk, or little walk within the neighborhood. This

---

[12] Under the Law of Attraction, the complete order of the Universe is determined, including everything that comes into your life and everything that you experience. It does so through the magnetic power of your thoughts. "Your thoughts become things!"— **Rhonda Byrne, author of the book, "The Secret".**

[13] The word **omnipotent** made its way into English through Anglo-French, but it ultimately derives from the Latin prefix omni-, meaning "all," and the word potens, meaning "potent." Its original applications in English referred specifically to the power held by an almighty God. —Merriam-Webster Dictionary

helps keep your blood pressure and heart rate at a steady but normal level. Getting started with a healthy breakfast is also a good habit. If you are tired of hearing that breakfast is important to your day, start eating healthy food instead. It helps you reach your goals and avoid making fast food choices. This habit can be established if you usually wake up early to get ready for the day's grind. It lets you to prepare a meal before heading out the door.

- **Manage your activities and set daily goals.** One important habit that you should develop is activity management. Your activities are easier to manage than managing time. If you tend to set a to-do list with a specified time in each, you will just be frustrated. Instead, try listing your priority activities and finish them according to importance. This discipline will help you maximize your time and achieve success in life. It does so by developing a strategy and implementing it effectively. There are many goals that everyone has. Whether business related or personal, everyone has. We all have a tendency to set long-term goals. However, setting short-term goals can help you develop a plan that works for you at the moment. It can be a lifesaver, motivating you to reach new goals and overcome obstacles with bigger tasks.

- **Read and learn every day.** Reading gave me a chance to learn new things and become a better person, and it has also taught me to be more intentional about all that I do. Good reading habits are the key to becoming more successful in life. Learning how to cultivate them will help you reach your goals faster. Learning new things helps keep the brain active. Just like muscles, the brain also has to be reflexed to develop new connections. There is also a lot more we get from learning new things than just making the brain stronger, and that makes us become happier and wiser.

- **Track your net worth and prepare your personal budgets.** Getting a bit of math can help you evaluate and plan for the future. Your Net worth reflects your financial position. It can also help you set goals and determine how to manage your financial health. Also, plan out your shopping activities. Having a list will help you avoid making an impulse purchase and buying something that doesn't really need to be bought. Before buying anything online, figure out what you really need and how much you can afford to spend. It will also keep you avoid making a mistake for non-essential items. Understanding these concepts can help you evaluate your financial situation and determine how to reach your goals. (*Net Worth and Budgeting were discussed in the next segments.*)

- **Pay yourself first.** Creating a budget is important, but pay yourself first if you want to save for the future. This helps you reach your saving goals and avoid running into debt. If you only pay yourself after taking care of your bills and expenses, you run the problem of not saving enough to hit your goals. A consistent good practice of contributing to savings is vital for building long-term wealth and providing a cushion for emergenciesa and investing. You may allocate 50% on needs, 30% on wants, and keep 20% to savings and investments. Or you may allocate depending on your financial objectives.

- **Invest wisely.** *Never invest money that you cannot afford to lose.* This is an impotant rule to follow when investing. Unfortunately, a lot of the time, people fail to discuss investing with their current circumstances. This is because they tend to overlook the importance of it for the future. (*Investing was discussed in the next segments*).

- **Track your financial progress.** Set aside sometime each month to track how much progress you've made in your financial goals. It will guide you on the right financial path. Also, Knowing how much debt you have paid off and how much progress you are making on saving and investing will help you keep on track. It will keep you boosted and motivated.

## Determining Your Financial Net Worth

Your net worth shows how much you can realistically accomplish in achieving major financial goals.[14] It also shows how much you can save for unexpected expenses.

It tells how much money you have to spend to achieve a specific financial target, such as paying off debts or buying a home.

Your financial assets (or everything you owned that has monetary value) minus your financial obligations (or the amounts you owe to others) is your Net Worth (or your financial wealth):

$$F.A. - F.O. = N.W.$$

The following segments explain how to determine those numbers. You may use any spreadsheet apps to tally them all.

### Add up Your Financial Assets

A financial asset is an investment that you can use to purchase something now or in the future.[15] This asset usually includes your money in various accounts, stocks, bonds, and mutual funds.

Money in your retirement saving accounts and the value of any businesses and real estate that you own are included in this calculation.

---

[14] **Net worth** signifies your wealth. It is the measure of your financial worth. (Garman & Forgue, 2018. Personal Finance, Thirteenth Edition, Cengage Learning, pg. 81);(Kapoor et. Al, 2019. Personal Finance: An active Approach to Help you Achieve Financial Literacy, McGraw Hill Education, pg. 48). **An individual's net worth** is simply the value that is left after subtracting liabilities from assets. (https://www.investopedia.com/terms/n/networth.asp)

[15] **A financial asset** is a liquid asset that gets its value from a contractual right or ownership claim like cash, stocks, bonds, mutual funds, bank deposits, etc. (Garman & Forgue, 2018. Personal Finance, Thirteenth Edition, Cengage Learning, pg. 80);(Kapoor et. Al, 2019. Personal Finance: An active Approach to Help you Achieve Financial Literacy, McGraw Hill Education, pg. 49)

Ideally, you would like to add a portion of the equity you plan to use to the list of assets. Your assets are divided into three categories: Monetary Assets, Tangible Assets, and Investment Assets.

Your monetary assets are your liquid assets or cash equivalents. You use these for your living expenses, emergencies, savings, and payment of bills.

Your tangible assets are your personal and real properties. Personal properties provide maintenance to your lifestyles like vehicles, gadgets, smartphones, and other movable properties. Real properties are those that are permanent, like a house, condominium. Take note that these tangible assets depreciate in value over time.

Your investment assets or otherwise known as capital assets, are financial rights that you own. They have a long life, generate income, and appreciate value over time like stocks, bonds, mutual funds, precious metals, real estate, and business. You may also include Social Security and pension payments.

Table 2.1 explains how to account for these monthly benefits when tallying your financial assets.

**TABLE 2.1 Your Financial Assets**

| Accounts | Value |
|---|---|
| **MONETARY ASSETS** | |
| Cash (Cash on hand, Bank accounts, Time deposits, and Receivables to others) | ₱_____ |
| Example: Bank Accounts | |
| Checking Account | ₱_____ |
| Savings Accounts | ₱_____ |
| *Subtotal* | ₱_____ |
| **TANGIBLE ASSETS** | |
| Smartphone/s & Jewelry | ₱_____ |
| Vehicle/s | ₱_____ |
| House, Condominium, Appliances, and Furniture | ₱_____ |
| *Subtotal* | ₱_____ |
| **INVESTMENT ASSETS** | |
| Stocks | ₱_____ |
| Real Estate (Land, House, Condo, and Car for rent) | ₱_____ |

| | |
|---|---|
| ETF/Currencies | ₱ |
| Mutual Funds | ₱ |
| Precious Metals | ₱ |
| NFT/Cryptocurrencies | ₱ |
| Business/es | ₱ |
| *Subtotal* | ₱ |
| **Benefits earned that pay a monthly premium:** | |
| Philhealth | ₱ |
| Social Security | ₱ |
| PAG-IBIG | ₱ |
| *Subtotal* | ₱ |
| **Total Financial Assets (add all subtotals)** | ₱ |

Suppose you are planning to retire in 20 years. In that case, your money from a different savings account should be converted into a total amount. However, suppose you are expecting inflation to reduce the value of your retirement. Therefore, you should consider that concern now.

Consumer items, such as your clothes, do not count as an asset unless you sell them, take note, you cannot live comfortably without them.

## Subtract Your Financial Obligations

To measure your financial net worth, you must subtract your financial obligation from your assets. Your financial obligation is the sum of all of your debts, including short-term loans and credit card debts.[16]

When figuring your debts, you should include money you borrowed from other people. Also, include debt that's owed on other real estate assets.

---

[16] **Financial Liabilities** or Financial Obligations, include both personal and business-related debts. It does not include items not yet due like next month's rent. (Garman & Forgue, 2018. Personal Finance, Thirteenth Edition, Cengage Learning, pg. 80-81); (Kapoor et. Al, 2019. Personal Finance: An active Approach to Help you Achieve Financial Literacy, McGraw Hill Education, pg. 50-51). **Financial obligations** represent any outstanding debts or regular payments that a party must make like if you owe or will owe money to anybody, that is one of your financial obligations. (https://www.investopedia.com/terms/o/obligation.asp)

If you include mortgage debts on your home as a liability, then have the home's value in your liability list.

Your liability can be short-term or long-term. All liabilities payable within a year shall be included in your short-term list. At the same time, the long-term items that are payable for more than a year shall be included in your long-term list.

## Consolidate Your Numbers

Here comes the little depressing part — reckoning out your debts and loans in Table 2.2.

**TABLE 2.2 Financial Obligations**

| Accounts | Balance |
|---|---|
| **SHORT-TERM OBLIGATIONS** | |
| Personal loans owed to others | |
| Consumer loans | |
| Bank credit card | ₱ |
| Past due rent or unpaid bills | ₱ |
| Other short term loans | ₱ |
| *Subtotal* | ₱ |
| **LONG-TERM OBLIGATIONS** | |
| Vehicle Loans | ₱ |
| Mortgages | ₱ |
| Home loans | ₱ |
| *Subtotal* | ₱ |
| **Total Financial Obligations (add all subtotals)** | ₱ |

After cracking all your numbers, deduct your financial obligations from your financial assets to get your net worth in Table 2.3.

**TABLE 2.3 Your Net Worth**

| Accounts | Balance |
|---|---|
| Total Financial Assets (from Table 2.1) | ₱ |
| Total Financial Obligations (from Table 2.2) | – ₱ |
| Net Worth | ₱ |

## Interpreting Your Net Worth Results

Your net worth is only useful to you if you have specific goals and circumstances in mind. A lot of people with high expectations might feel that their lifestyle is a small thing.

Your net worth can be amplified by increasing your financial assets and decreasing your financial obligations. Or, you may use your financial obligations to invest in a vehicle that generates a higher rate of return than the debt's interest rate.

If your net worth is less than it should be, it is time to start taking action. On the other hand, if it is still high, it is also time to reassess your financial situation.

# Examining Your Credit Score and Reports

Probably, you know that you have a credit report and a credit score. However, most of the time, obtaining these reports and scores is not an easy task. You may confer to your bank and request a representative therein to provide such documents.

A credit report contains information about your identities, such as your name, address, social security number, and account details. This data can be used to establish a record of your credit accounts. On the other hand, your credit score is a digital score derived from your credit report. It tells lenders if you are most likely to default on your debts.[17]

## Improve Your Credit Reports and Score

Instead of just buying credit scores or paying for monitoring services, try improving your credit score instead. There are many advantages

---

[17] **Credit Report** or credit file refers to the record of your complete credit history. Your **Credit Score** summarizes your credit history and reflects the information in your credit report. It is the snapshot of your credit report at the time it is calculated. (Kapoor et. Al, 2019. Personal Finance: An active Approach to Help you Achieve Financial Literacy, McGraw Hill Education, pg. 153-157)

of having a good credit score, like fast approval of business loans and emergency loans.

Here are the most critical ways that you may consider to boost your reputation to lenders:

- **At least gather your three credit reports, and make sure they are correct.** Make sure to collect all your accounts and data. If you are planning to borrow, your credit reports will determine if you have a chance or not.
- **Pay all your bills on time.** Being responsible in paying your bills will save you a lot of money. If you are preoccupied with many schedules, you may install mobile apps for automatic payment of bills. Automatic bills payment is a service that many companies offer to help keep your accounts on time. Pay bills on time to save you from penalties and to increase your credit rating.
- **Choose options that don't cost you.** Doing so will help boost your credit score. For example, If you can refinance your home loan and save some money, then do so. Likewise, if you have high-interest credit card debt and want to transfer it to a lower-rate card, then it is more convenient.
- **Limit your debt and debt accounts.** You should limit the number of loans and bills you carry out to improve your credit score. It is also important to keep the balances low enough to avoid getting into high debt. Manage your debt accounts well.

If you aim for a good credit rating, you must use credit wisely. For the long term, your responsible credit behavior is one of the effective ways to improve your scores.

Here are some information used to measure your credit score:

- The type of accounts you have like credit cards, auto loans, and mortgages
- On-time payment of bills
- Available credit you are using currently

- Amount of your outstanding debt
- The maturity of your debt and age of your accounts

## Bad Debt Versus Good Debt

Usually, people borrow money to finance the cost of a college education. Since they don't have enough money to cover the entire cost, borrowing money helps them finance their education.

A new car is a great way to spend money, but what if you don't have the money to buy it? Should you finance it for how many years?

The people, dealers, or banks who were eager to offer you a car loan say that you deserve it and that you can afford it. In reality, they are asking you to borrow away from them plus interests to get a better deal.

Spending more than you can afford on vacation will make your money go away. Even if you have fond memories of the trip, it is not worth the money. Of course, I'm not suggesting that you avoid taking a vacation. Still, I believe that if you can afford it, then take the break you can afford. If not, then you might as well save for it or not taking it at all.

## Consuming Your Way To Bad Debt

Bad debt is a term that refers to the excess amount of money that people accumulate for consumption. It is very harmful to their long-term financial health.

If you save enough in advance, you'll be able to take more vacations each year. But, unfortunately, if you borrow and pay off all of the interest on your debts, you'll end up with less money for other goals.

The huge interest rates charged by banks and other financial institutions on consumer loans are reasons why people have difficulty saving money. But, I'm not saying that everyone should never borrow. Instead, I suggest that people use good debt to purchase real estate or start a new business.

If managed properly, these investments can increase in value. Good debts can be rationalized through proper moderation and proper acquisition of quality assets.

## Identifying Bad Debt Overload

Do you have debt that is relative to your yearly income? How much? Doing so can help you figure out how much debt you have and what its worth. Assessing how much debt you have is a useful tool to size up your debts. In addition, it can help you avoid accruing bad debts.

Bad debt is a loan that you use to purchase things that depreciate in value. Divide your annual income by your bad debt to calculate the danger ratio.

$$\frac{Bad\ Debt}{Annual\ Income} = Bad\ debt\ danger\ ratio$$

The amount of bad debt that people carry is zero. So never buy anything with a credit card that you cannot afford to pay off at the end of the month.

Not everybody may agree with me. For instance, one of the major credit card companies I use to teach students about money management says that carrying a huge debt is fine. It is correct for as long as the debt is used to buy an asset that produces a steady cash flow.

Your bad debt danger ratio over 25 percent can have real trouble. It can get out of control without intervention. The growth of debt can get out of control unless something significant is done to prevent it.

How much good debt is acceptable depends on many factors. In this segment, we shall determine how much savings you need to save to reach your goals.

Borrow money only for investments that can increase in value over the long term. This includes buying things that retain their original value and grow in value. Don't borrow money for consumption, as these will eventually become worthless. Instead, borrow for something that will increase in value and become financially worthy.

## Weighing Good Debt: How Much Can You Get?

Like good food, good debt can also be harmful. When it comes to investing, debt can be a good thing or a bad one.

There is no magic formula to determine when you have too much debt. Mostly, it comes down to being too focused on debt and not paying it off.

With a few questions, you can talk about the debts weighing on you and your loved ones. These are the few most important questions to ask yourself if you're in debt.

- Are you and your loved ones sleeping well at night so that they can function properly the next month?
- Are the rewards worth the risk? If so, then you should consider taking out a loan. If not, then you should not borrow.

Here are ways on how you could get out of excessive debt:

- Regulate your account balances and the payments required. Always take note of the interest rates and the additional fees, penalties, and surcharges.
- Don't use debt to pay another debt. This will create a domino effect, especially if you are paying a debt from consumption. It will just be a continuous cycle. If you used a debt with a lower interest rate to repay a debt with a higher one, it could be better. But again, take note that if the debt is not used to generate income, it will still be a great problem.
- Increase your income. Consider ways to create passive income or other sources aside from your current one. If you are employed, make a side hustle. Don't stop creating income streams. Even if it earns 200 pesos a day, that will be 6000 pesos a month extra income. It is just a number game. The greater streams of income you have, the more cash flow you can make.

## Analyzing Your Savings

How much have you saved financially in the past year?

Some people have no idea how much they are saving or how much they are spending. The trick is to determine the amount of money they have leftover after a year. To better understand their financial situation, it is important to calculate their net worth.

The amount you saved last year is equivalent to the change in your Net Worth over the past year.

If you own a house, ignore this advice. Instead, consider the extra payments you make on your mortgage each month and the savings you make from these.

If you have already computed your net worth from a year ago, you should correctly do the exercise in Table 2.4. However, if you want to know how much savings you have, you need to do a few more calculations.

For example, one year ago, you bought 100 shares of a stock at ₱17 per share. Today, the value of your investment is ₱34 per share. This ₱1,700 increase in value is not saved and should be removed from your calculations. I'm not penalizing you for your smart investments, but I also get to add back the value of those less successful ones.

**TABLE 2.4 Your Savings Capacity**

| Step 1: Figure out your savings | | | |
|---|---|---|---|
| Today | | One Year Ago | |
| Savings & investments | ₱___ | Savings & investments | ₱___ |
| – Obligations | ₱___ | – Obligations | ₱___ |
| Net worth today | ₱___ | Net worth 1 year ago | ₱___ |
| Step 2: Adjust changes in the value of your investments during the year | | | |
| Net worth today | | | ₱___ |
| – Net worth 1 year ago | | | ₱___ |
| – Appreciation of investments (past year) | | | ₱___ |

| | | | |
|---|---|---|---|
| + Depreciation of investments (past year) | | | ₱____ |
| **Savings rate** | | | ₱____ |

If you're not comfortable with the numbers, try this simple approach: *Save a portion of your monthly income.* This method works for everyone.

How much money do you keep in a month? Get the statements for your accounts to see how much you're contributing to each month. For example, you're not really saving if you save for a few months and then spend it on auto repairs. Also, if you depleted an old savings account, don't count it as new savings.

Save at least 5 to 20% of your annual income for long-term financial goals, such as retirement or travel goals. This step can help you set up a plan to save more.

## Your Investment Knowledge

If you're with me through the first couple of chapters, then you've already completed the challenging part of this chapter.

Whether you have a small amount or a large sum of money to invest, it is important to understand the rights and wrongs associated with investing.

Having the proper knowledge about investing can help you manage your money well into the future. In addition, knowing how much time you need to dedicate to investing can help determine how much time you can spare. Finally, having answered yes or no to these questions will help determine how much time you should spend learning about investment:

- Are you aware that there are risks involved in investing?
- Is it worth tapping into in the event of a sudden emergency?
- Do people outside of retirement accounts understand how these types of investments can generate income and gains?

- Do you have money in different types of investments that are not dependent on one or a few specific securities (like bonds, stocks, real estate, and so on)?
- Are you planning on having a major expenditure in the following years, and will you put all of your money into conservative investments instead of risky ones?
- Are you investing for long-term goals that are likely to generate higher returns than inflation?
- Do you know how to evaluate a stock?
- If you are currently investing in stocks, do you know how to evaluate a company's financial statements and competitive position?
- Do you know how to review the company's balance sheet, income statement, competitive position, price-earnings ratio versus its peer group, and so on?
- If you work with a financial adviser, do you understand what they are recommending and are comfortable with the actions that they are taking?

Not having the proper tools and strategies to make and save money is not guaranteed of financial success. Instead, it can lead to the same end result as not saving at all. You may not be able to enjoy the money that you have lost, but you will certainly feel guilty about it.

## Your Insurance Knowledge

This section will help you manage the various aspects of protecting yourself and your assets. The following questions will help you answer these questions.

- Do your current insurance policies make sense for your financial situation?
- Do you understand the various types of insurance policies that cover multiple aspects of your personal life?
- If your family depends on you financially, do you have enough life insurance coverage to replace your income if you die?

- Do you know that it makes sense to buy life insurance through a fee-for-service advisor or companies that sell directly to the public?
- Do you have liability insurance for your car, home, or business?

If you answered yes to all of the questions correctly, then you probably feel good about yourself. In the following segments, you will learn how to avoid making major mistakes when buying insurance.

# Chapter 3
# Creating and Reaching Goals

---

*Shoot for the moon. Even if you miss, you'll land among the stars.*
*–Les Brown*

---

As a finance instructor, I asked friends and students their long- and short-term financial goals. Of course, it is incredibly valuable to them, but they were not so excited anymore because of their current financial state. Instead, they think that life is challenging and seemingly hopeless.

I help you dream about what you want to happen in life and how money fits it in this segment. Then, it will help you make the most of every money you have.

Most of us have our own picture of success. However, according to John C. Maxwell, two things are required towards the success journey: *the right picture of success and the correct principles for getting there.* To him, success is knowing your purpose in life, growing to reach your maximum potential, and sowing seeds that benefit others. [18]

Remember that the greater value you offer to many, the greater wealth that will get back to you. You may get me wrong, but I am saying that becoming wealthy in all aspects of Life (Physically, Mentally, Emotionally, Socially, and Spiritually) would speak of our great success. Unfortunately, wealth is one of the most misunderstood words linked to success. Wealth in money doesn't guarantee success. It is just a part of it.

---

[18] **John C. Maxwell**, a #1 New York Times bestselling author, motivational speaker, leadership guru and pastor. He also developed the 5 levels of leadership, which visualize at which level a leader perform and how she or he can be more influential, respected and successful. He has sold more than 26 million books in fifty languages and was identified as the #1 leader in business by the American Management Association® and the most influential leadership expert in the world by Business Insider and Inc. magazine.

Ancient Greek Millionaire Aristotle Onassis recognized that money isn't the same as success. He said that *after you reach a certain point, money becomes unimportant. What matters is a success.*[19]

Before diving into the setting and saving for common financial goals, you must define wealth and success clearly.

## Articulate the Right Definition of Wealth

*The more people with money, the more attention they get.* This obsession with wealth seems to have become mainstream. This is evidenced by the various rankings that are released by various publications.

My years of working experience, interviews of business people, and readings from the books about wealth and the wealthy had convinced me that there's a slight correlation between wealth and emotional wealth. So, it is important to remember that the pursuit of financial security and wealth comes with many emotional sides.

We create a living by what we acquire, but we make a life by what we offer. One essential part of being wealthy is helping others. The more people you help and serve, the more income you get. Financial success is all about finding your passion and helping others while you are pursuing it. Success is not dependent on what you get or achieve for yourself but on what you do for others. Some are earning vast amounts of money because they are helping or serving others. They create businesses to create employment, then from that, income follows.

### Money Can't Buy Everything

Remember the times when you thought about the best moments in your life? Probably won't include the time you got a car. The old saying is true: *The most valuable things in your life can't be bought.* Unfortunately, too many people act as if money can buy happiness. It

---

[19] **Aristotle Onassis**, a Greek shipping magnate who developed a fleet of supertankers and freighters larger than the navies of many countries. and a wealthy international celebrity. (https://www.greekschannel.com/aristotle-onassis-the-life-of-the-world-s-richest-greek-tycoon/)

is tempting to believe that money can buy happiness, as it can increase one's enjoyment of life.

Researches show that the link between money and happiness is not as strong as we think. According to psychologist David Myers, wealth can also cause misery, even though it's not a guarantee of happiness.[20] So despite all the advanced gadgets and luxuries people claim to make life better, people still aren't as happy as years ago.

## Keep it Balanced

Some people are too lazy to save enough. In my Personal Finance classes, I often see my students who are unsure about their financial future. I also see people who are too focused on saving too much and forget to take care of their health. Saving might give you your goal, but you will be consumed by time. It is not just supposed to be saving alone; it should be accompanied by investing.

People who are trying to save for an ultimate goal can get consumed by their saving habits. Sometimes, they make too many sacrifices today while trying to get some vision of their future. Others get so consumed by work that they forget about their families and friends.

One of the problems with wealth is that it can take decades for people to realize that they don't have to work all that much to be happy. If you make happiness your goal, you certainly will fail all the time. Happiness is a choice; always choose it. Never consider it as your only measure of success.

One of the costs of working is time spent away from family and friends. Having too much time away from them can be very costly.

Of course, at the other extreme are wasters who live only for today. A friend of mine once said, *You only live once* or *Why save when we will all die?* which seems to be the mottos of this personality type. It's not

---

[20] https://davidmyers.org/books/the-pursuit-of-happiness/

actually bad, but he might just overspent every day without thinking for the future.

This approach can make people lax, lazy, or take money for granted, a *one day millionaire*, as they want to work for a living and spend all they earn in a day. It may also make them work till they are old.

If you can't work or have little money to live on, it can be a tragic situation. Most people will eventually get homeless. To earn and save money is like eating. If you eat less, you become malnourished. If you eat much, it will make you overweight and unhealthy. The right amount of money can help you have a healthy, balanced, and peaceful existence. However, it should be treated with respect.

Being satisfied isn't so much about what you want as it is about what you have. According to Dr. David Myers, being rich isn't about having everything that you want. It is about being able to live with what you have. There are ways to make the most of what you make. [21]

Check out these ways of becoming rich: First, have a wealthy mindset and abundant means; Second, decide and act consistently. Discover ways to make money while you sleep, keep your feet on the ground, and humble up. Don't lose sight of all that is far more important than money.

## *Your Saving Goals Inventory*

Most people have life and financial goals. This part will discuss the most common ones and how to get them. Check whether any of the following reflect your ambitions:

- **Owning real estate properties:** Getting into the real estate market is a great way to create wealth for a lifetime. Despite

---

[21] **Dr. David G. Myers**, an internationally renowned scientist, author, and teacher whose research and writing have covered a wide range of topics, including group behavior, prejudice, personality, religion, intuition, hearing loss, and personal well-being.

the recent decline in property prices, it is still a long-term investment if you lease it and rent it out.

- **Retiring/Achieving financial independence:** Retiring doesn't involve sitting on a rocking chair. It's about living comfortably and achieving financial freedom. It means living happily and not working for pay. Some people find it more satisfying than working full time.
- **Educating the kids:** Teach your kids the basics of saving and investing. Don't feed them the different money mistakes discussed in the first part of this book. Instead, give them enough time to tour the city, visit a museum, or take educational trips to ensure that they enjoy being educated well.
- **Owning your business:** Many people dream about owning their business, but the reality is that it requires a lot of work and emotional control. Even with the right amount of start-up capital, many people often struggle to maintain their standard of living while expanding their businesses. Just Push it.

Because everyone has their own unique goals, achieving them can be challenging. However, setting and achieving goals that are specific to you can be done on their own. Some ways to do this are expanding your cash flow streams, saving, and investing money.

## Important Things to You

You can't afford to spend lavishly on luxuries unless you have a large family financial inheritance. To ensure that you have enough resources to live comfortably, prioritize your goals.

One common mistake people make is entering a financial decision without fully considering the important things. As a financial management professional, I can tell you that people who do their goals and then work towards them are typically the most successful at achieving them.

## Prioritize Your Goals

If you intend to buy a house or start a business, you may need to save some money before you reach age 60. However, even if you're not yet retired, you still have to pay income taxes on the money you withdraw. Because you can't rely solely on savings, it is important to set goals for yourself, invest your money as early as possible.

# Save to Buy a House or Business

Deciding whether to save for a home or build a business can be a scary financial decision. But, in the long run, most especially if you have multiple sources of income, owning a home and buying significant purchases will be easy.

If you aim to buy a house, then you must save before retirement. However, if you're not ready to start buying a house yet, then put off saving until after retirement. Or you may want to buy a home, mortgage it, lease it out, and let the lease payments pay for the mortgage. Sounds fun, right?

Most people have the same problem when saving for a house or starting a new business. The same goes for people who are planning on buying a house.

Instead of putting your money in a bank account, start investing in your own small business. This strategy can help you avoid making big mistakes and enjoying the rewards of being a small-business owner and long-term investor.

## Develop Your Savings/ Investment Strategy

Money going toward retirement can include both cash in a retirement account and cash in a non-retirement account. You can also invest in non-retirement accounts such as stocks and bonds. You can also include the difference between the sale price and the amount owed on a mortgage in rental or investment properties.

Equity in your home is a difficult decision to make. If you want to take advantage of it in retirement, don't include it in your savings when you tally up all of your assets. You may want to consider a portion of your home's equity to take advantage of it as you retire. Some people sell their houses when they retire and move closer to family or economize.

## Value Your Time

Winners fight and aim to win while losers fight not to lose. So, if you're not sure how to start saving, here are some tips to help you get started:

- **Strategize your spending.** There are two basic ways to boost your savings: First, earn more money or cut your spending. Doing both will increase your savings. Second, Don't spend money not earned yet.
- **Be more realistic about your retirement age.** You can extend your retirement age by a couple of years if you want to. It will allow you to save more and spend less. If your job makes you crazy, try looking for passive income ideas or side hustle during your early retirement years. This will help make you happy and relieve stress.
- **Get your investments growing.** You can get more out of your assets by investing in them at a faster rate. It helps you reach your goals earlier. Earning a few extra points a year can significantly reduce the amount you need to save. For example, if you're in your 30's and your investments have appreciated at a faster pace than inflation, the total you'll need to save each month for retirement drops by around 40 percent.
- **Turn a hobby into supplemental retirement income.** Even if you don't plan on working for long, turning a hobby into an additional income can be done for many reasons. One of these is to develop a business plan. First, get started with a business plan and pick something that interests you. Then, get smart about how to market and sell your goods and services. Be resourceful and innovative! You never know life until you make it— you might turn your passion into a business publication!

# Chapter 4
# Money Come and Go

---

*Spending money to show people how much money
you have is the fastest way to have less money.*
— Morgan Housel, The Psychology of Money

---

As a finance teacher and financial consultant, I have encountered people who have varying incomes. There are three main categories: low-to-moderate income, mid-to-high income, and high-end income.

- People spending more than their earnings (accumulating debt or credit)
- People who are spending all that they earn (saving nothing — breaking even)
- People saving 2, 5, 10, or even 20 percent or more (growing savings)

The Philippine Institute for Development Studies (PIDS) recognized social classes according to the following income brackets in the Philippines:[22]

- **Poor:** Below ₱10,957 monthly income
- **Low-income but not poor:** ₱10,957 to ₱21,914 monthly income
- **Lower middle:** ₱21,914 to ₱43,828 monthly income
- **Middle:** ₱43,828 to ₱76,669 monthly income
- **Upper middle:** ₱76,669 to ₱131,484 monthly income
- **Upper middle but not rich:** ₱131,483 to ₱219,140 monthly income
- **Rich:** ₱219,140 and above monthly income

I've seen people who make over ₱2,000,000 a year save less than ₱1,000,000, while those who make more than that save nothing.

---

[22]  https://pids.gov.ph/

You currently earn ₱2,500,000 a year, and you spend all of it. If you live comfortably but still have a few bills to pay, then maybe you should try living below your income. Also, probably increase your ideas on how to create multiple streams of income.

Many people live on less than they make. If they spend as they do, they can save and invest the difference. This segment explains why people tend to overspend and avoid making the same mistake in the future. It will help and guide you to live a better life and save more.

It is also possible that living in a place that costs so much makes you feel like you have no control over your expenses. It may be true that moving to a more advantageous location can save you money. Still, it can also get you thinking about other options.

## Examining Overspending

If it is your first time managing your money, you must live within your means to reach your goals. Doing so requires saving less than you earn and investing your savings intelligently.

Putting yourself in a better financial position, take a look at your spending habits. It can be effortless to get carried away with the notion that you should spend more than you make.

Most of the time, the influences in society encourage people to spend. As a result, you are often referred to as a consumer or a member of the government. This section aims to look at some of the adversaries you face when controlling spending.

## Accessing Credit

With the rise of digital currencies and mobile apps, it is easier to spend money. Unfortunately, most people get into debt because they make purchases that they can't afford when it comes to credit. This is typically the reason why many people get into debt.

## Using Credit Cards Wisely

Credit cards are convenient for getting goods and services if you pay your bills in full each month. However, if you carry a high amount of debt, they can make it hard to live beyond your means.

Suppose you keep charging on your credit card and making only the minimum monthly payment. In that case, you'll end up a delinquent debtor. You will not be able to pay off the debt. Your high-interest debts will keep piling up.

Some credit cards are now offering insurance that they can use to cover the minimum payments for the months that a debtor can't pay. However, this type of card usually comes with a higher annual interest rate than the typical card. So if you have a tendency to charge up a storm and spend more than you should with those plastic cards, then you should get rid of them.

## Evaluating Car loans

Getting into a car is as easy as walking into a dealership and buying one that's not going to cost you much. Monthly payments are typically low enough to allow you to afford a new vehicle.

You hear people around say, *Stop using your old car. It's time to get a new one, Oh come on! Reward yourself,* or *You have a stable job, you can afford the mortgage.*

You start looking around at all the new cars, and then the car dealer explains everything to you; like, there it is your new car. It's clean and elegant, and it has all the latest features and comforts. Car dealers were not exactly sure what the fine print is, but they'll always make you feel like you're getting a bargain. They'll always make you talk about the car's attractive features and the benefits of getting one.

After a test drive, you think, *How can I afford this car?* You then realize that, despite all the luxuries that come with it, it only costs you ₱15,000 a month. You thought that the price was already bad. Before you know it, the dealer checks your credit report and has you sign a few papers.

The salesman wants you to think about monthly payments because the cost of a car sounds so cheap. However, it's actually ₱15,000 a month for many months. What does the total sticker price of a car come out to when interest charges are included in? How much are the maintenance and insurance costs of your vehicle over the next seven years or more? What if you are just earning enough and don't have any other source of income? Now you're probably sacrificing more than a year's worth of your income. That hurts.

## Going Out for Recreations

You go out with some friends and plan to spend some time together. However, since you have a budget, it can be challenging to determine which event would be most affordable for you.

Some people are so focused on the latest movies, music, or technology that they forget about the past. They don't want to feel left behind.

The idea that you can just deal with the here-and-now is beautiful. But unfortunately, it leads people to rationalize not having long-term goals and needs. This mindset leads people to spend their lives in jobs that they dislike, and it can keep them stuck in them for a long time.

You may feel that tomorrow is not coming, but living for today has its virtues. Your spending habits should be based on what you want and plan on. Not everyone has the same goals and plans. This helps you save more than you initially thought.

## Spending Money to Feel Good

Most people say that life is full of demands and stress. So it is not unusual for people to work hard and deserve to indulge in some time. You're working hard for everything you get, and it shows how much effort you put into making sure that your work is done well. But as a result, spending more than you deserve is a sign that you're not working hard enough to deserve it.

Like people who smoke cigarettes, drink alcohol, or become addicted to the Internet, some individuals also become addicted to spending.

Researchers can identify psychological causes of a spending addiction, like how parents handled money.[23] Money habits can be tracked based on each money blueprint. These were molded during a person's growth. Others may have experienced living with parents who are full of vices, gambling, and overspending. These circumstances and the wrong beliefs about money discussed in the first chapter hold people back from abundance.

## Scrutinizing Your Spending

A fit and diverse diet, regular exercise, and brushing your teeth are all good habits. But, like some of these habits, saving enough and investing for the long term are some practices that can help you save and improve your wealth appetite. Building multiple sources of income can also help keep you financially healthy and happy. These habits can also help you save for your future financial goals.

Despite having high incomes, many people have a hard time saving enough for a good portion of their income. This is typically due to their excessive spending. Check these spending analyses if any of them are applicable in your life:

- You want to meet your financial goals, but you aren't saving enough.
- You don't know where your income goes. Your spending is out of control.
- You are anticipating a major life adjustment like settling for marriage, having children, building a business, retiring, and so on.

---

[23] (A) https://blackbearrehab.com/mental-health/behavioral-processaddictions/compulsive-buying-disorder/causes/ (B) https://www.psychguides.com/behavioral-disorders/shopping-addiction/

If you already have a good savings mentality, then you may not need to do this analysis. However, if you have goals and are already tracking your spending, I don't see much value in this process.

You have already established the good habit of saving. But, do not track exactly where you spend all of your money each month.

Knowing where your money goes is very helpful, as it can help you set goals and make changes in how you spend and save. It can also help you save more money and meet those goals. Practice budgeting. Having a budget isn't about keeping track of how much you spend each month. It's about saving what you need to achieve your goals.

## *Manual Spending Tracker*

Analyzing spending is like being a detective. First, you collect clues to reconstruct the spending habits of others. You can get all the details you need to keep track of every single transaction. To get started, get out/access your:

- **Spending Receipts**
- **ITR (Income Tax Returns)**
- **Banking Statement/s**
- **Bills payment record**
- **Record of checks issued and paid**
- **Monthly debit card reports**
- **Credit card bills and transactions**

Ideally, you want to track 12 months of your spending. But, if your habits change over time, or if you're unsure how to sum up your purchases, you can reduce the amount of data you collect to six months or less.

When planning for a significant gift or vacation, make sure that you include the months when you spend a lot of money. Also, account for insurance that you may choose to pay monthly. Most of the time, keeping a record of all the transactions made with cash is challenging since it doesn't leave a paper trail. But you may consider receipts if there are.

You can also try estimating how much you spend on free websites and apps each month. This will automatically keep track of your spending habits. For example, track your online shopping transactions, how much you spend, and how often you buy.

You can also try adding up all the cash transactions from your checking account if there are. Then, use Table 3.1 to separate your spending into various categories. Again, it's a good idea to keep all of your spendings in mind so that it's clearly defined and useful.

Note: You may want to include your Social Security, PAG-IBIG, and Philhealth premiums paid every month.

## TABLE 3.1 Your Detailed Spending

| Category | Monthly Average (₱) | Percent of Total Gross Income (%) |
|---|---|---|
| **Lifestyle** | | |
| Rent | | |
| Mortgage | | |
| Utility Bills (Water & Electricity) | | |
| Phones | | |
| Internet & Movie Subscriptions | | |
| Appliances | | |
| Car Repairs and maintenance | | |
| **Food** | | |
| Dine-in and takeout | | |
| Gasoline | | |
| Clothing | | |
| Shoes | | |
| **Repayments** | | |
| Credit card charges | | |
| Auto loan | | |
| SSS, Philhealth & PAG-IBIG | | |
| **Recreations** | | |
| Entertainment (Tickets) | | |
| Travel | | |
| Gifts | | |
| Hobbies | | |
| Memberships | | |
| Pets | | |
| Other | | |

| Personal care | | |
|---|---|---|
| Haircuts | | |
| Personal hygiene | | |
| Health club or gym | | |
| Others | | |
| **Personal business** | | |
| Accountant | | |
| Legal Counsel | | |
| Others | | |
| **Health care** | | |
| Medicines | | |
| Dental | | |
| **Insurance** | | |
| Auto | | |
| Health | | |
| Life | | |
| **Educational expenses** | | |
| Tuition | | |
| Books | | |
| Supplies | | |
| Rental costs (bed & board) | | |
| **Children** | | |
| Daycare | | |
| Toys | | |
| **Charitable donations** | | |
| **Others** | | |

## Smart Track Your Spending

There are available tools that can help monitor your spending. These can help you keep track of all your bills and make it easier to pay them. They can also help you save a lot of money. You need to enter all the information that you pay with cash and credit card.

Most of us have difficulty saving money and reducing our spending. So this is no surprise that there is a wide range of free websites and apps that promise to help people accomplish these goals.

Several new sites are popping up all the time, and among them are PocketGuard, Personal Capital, YNAB- Budget, and others. For example, you may search Google play or Appstore and just type *Budget Tracker*, and many of them will pop out.

Personally, I created my Spending Tracker in an Excel file to monitor my money in and out. A pencil and paper may work well to keep track of your spending. Still, electronic devices such as smartphones and tablets are more useful tools for tracking bills and expenses. But again, both of them can work just fine. Find what fits you and what you are comfortable with.

# Part 2
## Spending Less, Saving More

Find out the wise ways to utilize your money.

Formulate strategies for reducing your spending.

Understand how to use credit and debt to create wealth.

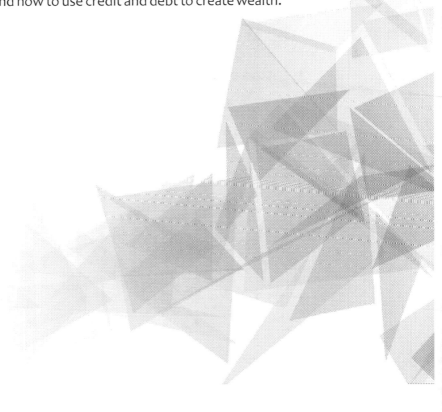

# Chapter 5
# Using Credit and Debt Prudently

---

*Never spend your money before you have it.*
*– Thomas Jefferson*

---

Accumulating bad debt by buying something that you can't afford is like being on a sugar and caffeine diet. It will be dangerous in the long term. Likewise, using a credit card to purchase a vacation is like eating an unbalanced diet. It's not healthy and can take away your long-term financial health.

When you borrow money to invest in the future, it's good debt. It is like eating a well-balanced diet. Not to say that you can't get into trouble when using good debt. However, just as with food, too much debt can induce financial indigestion.

In this chapter, getting rid of debts was discussed. It may be hard to do, but in the long run, it will pay off. I personally experienced it, and I learned it the hard way.

Before deciding which debt reduction strategies are right for you, you should evaluate your overall financial situation. Then, after you get out of bad debt, make sure to avoid credit problems in the future.

## Use Savings to Cut Your Consumer Debt

Many people have a mental brick wall that prevents them from looking at their various financial accounts in one place. You have to see your savings accounts and debts in the same view.

### Appreciate Your Gaining Power

If you have enough savings to pay off debts, such as credit card and auto loans, then pay them off first.

Even though you may be saving more than you intend to do, you still have to pay off your debts. Doing so will reduce the interest you're paying on your debts.

If paying off credit card debts is your goal, then paying Twelve percent isn't like finding an investment that promised Twelve percent returns. It is actually a higher-than-normal return that is required to justify not paying off the debts.

You would need an investment that yielded Eighteen percent to justify not paying off your Twelve percent loan. So even if you think you can make more money on investments, take the risk and pay down your debts.

To chase that higher potential return, you need to take a substantial risk. If you use your savings to settle your debts, make sure to leave enough of an emergency backup.

You want to be in an excellent financial position to endure an unexpected expense. However, if you use credit card debt to pay down balances, you may find yourself in a financial problem. It will be a continuous cycle over and over again.

## Using the Debt Cycle Wisely

Regardless of how you manage your debt, it is important to remember that paying off your debts is a risky endeavor. It will require you to think of alternatives and keep your emotions aligned with your goals. So it's not just how you manage debt but also how you deal with your emotional state.

### Resisting the Unnecessary Credit Temptation

These strategies will help you utilize debt properly, and I have included a list of other tactics that will help you get rid of credit card debts.

- **Don't increase your credit limit if you are not ready.** This is risky if you haven't mastered your emotions at spending yet. While figuring out how to control your spending habits, decrease your credit limit in the meantime. A high credit limit might be tempting if you can't manage it. The good thing about a high credit limit is that you can use your line of credit to fund properties or assets that generate income or cash flow. For example, you may use credit to invest in securities that earn a greater percentage than the interest payments or other investment vehicles that generate a higher rate of return.

- **Don't buy anything on credit that depreciates in value.** As much as possible, your necessities should not be purchased on credit. The minor expenses might be tolerable, but the major ones could lead to bad debt. Likewise, never borrow money for something that will depreciate in value. Instead, borrow money for sound investments such as Real Estate, Stocks, Bonds, Cryptocurrencies, or your own business.
- **Look at the entire picture.** Many people make purchases based on the monthly payments they can afford, like big Televisions, big Refrigerators, etc. It looks cheaper, but it's not. It is reasonable if you have sources of income, but if there's only one, then it is not. So it is important to know the total cost, including interest charges and other expenses.

# Chapter 6
# Reducing Your Spending

---

*You can have a Master's degree in making money, but you*
*will still wind up broke if you have a Ph.D. in spending it.*
*— Orrin Woodward*

---

I tried convincing people to spend their money wisely. I often had to tell them how to do it. This is a risky undertaking, as most people hate to be told what to do.

Building good money habits is the same as cutting you off from your comfort zones. The decision to cut is up to you. It's up to you to decide when you want to cut and change for the better. You should value your time by doing things that will contribute to your financial success.

The fact that you're being busy may also be a factor in how much money you spend. This chapter focuses on strategies that can help you save without taking up a lot of time.

## *Revealing the Keys to Responsible Spending*

For most people, spending money is much more fun than earning it. In fact, it is often easier to spend money than to earn it.

Many people tend to get carried away with details, which can lead to missing the big picture. In this part, I share my four fundamental principles for successful spending:

- Living within your means while expanding it.
- Finding the best values.
- Cutting off excessive expenditures.
- Using consumer credit properly.

## *Living within Your Means while Growing Your Net Worth*

Don't let the habits of others dictate yours. Instead, try adopting a different approach of spending less. For example, instead of spending lavishly on luxuries, try shopping with limited funds. This will help you keep away from paying more than you can afford.

How much you can safely spend depends on how much money you have leftover and your financial state. It means that you should save more than you make and avoid debt. It also means that you should never overextend yourself.

Living below or within your means could be good or bad advice. It is good if you are doing it while increasing your assets and building wealth. Going out of debt is also good but learn how to use it to increase your net worth. Use credit or debt wisely.

Most people often think that they can't afford to take on specific tasks. This is because they haven't figured out how they can afford them. Author Oscar Wilde quoted, *Anyone who lives within their means suffers from a lack of imagination.* [24] Imagination is limitless. Everything that existed was the product of our imaginations. Think outside of the box. Explore other ways to expand our net worth.

Author and Entrepreneur Robert Kiyosaki have two symbolic dads. His poor biological dad and his best friend's rich dad. He said that if he wanted something, his *poor dad* would always say, *we can't afford that*, which shuts down the possibility of getting what he desired. In contrast, his *rich dad* would tell him that if he can't afford it yet, he should think of possibilities to get it. [25]

Instead of saying *I can't* to achieve your objective, imagine how you could do it in a way that makes sense to you. Impossible just means that

---

[24] **Oscar Wilde**, Irish wit, poet, novelist and dramatist. To him, Imagination is a quality given to man to compensate for what he is not, and a sense of humaor is provided to console him from what he is.

[25] **Robert Kiyosaki** said that instead of living below your means, it's better for you to create means of earning more. Increasing your income is better than cutting back your expenses.

you haven't found the solution yet. The word *problem* exists because of the word *solution*.

It doesn't mean that you should go into debt. Instead, it means that you can live the life that you always wanted, with the help of a bit of ingenuity, of course.

It makes sense that people should save for certain expenses, such as paying off debts. But it's also a trick to suggest that people have to live below their means. Holding on to this concept without learning and growth is dangerous. Wealthy people expand their means by acquiring knowledge and more wisdom. From that, they create ways on how they can earn and acquire assets and build wealth.

## Consider the Best Values

You can find low cost and quality in the same product. But, unfortunately, quality products are usually the ones that come with a high price.

When evaluating a product or service, think about its long-term costs. For instance, if you buy the Second Hand Car for *Three Hubdred Thousand* (₱300,000) and then compare it to a brand new one which is *Seven Hundred Thousand* (₱700,000), you'll see that the brand new one requires a higher cost of ownership but will last long. But what if you only have enough? Practically, if you need a car and your savings and net worth cannot afford it yet, get a new car by paying a *Two Hundred Thousand* (₱200,000) down payment. Then, register it to *Grab* or other freelance deliveries for a side hustle. Then, invest the remaining *One Hundred Thousand* (₱100,000) in an asset that will give you a steady cash inflow to pay the installments so that your other source of income will not be compromised. People who sell certain products or services may initially appear to be your best interests at heart. However, this may change once they convince you to go with their advice.

## Focus on Quality & Affordability

Quality is important to you, but it also needs to be maintained at a fair price. Advertising is a good business practice. However, it is important to consider companies' products and services first. It is maybe good to look at brands, but if there are products that match the quality and will cost you less, go for it, why not?

If a product labeled as *store brand* is located to one another, the prices of both products are the same. So not only are they spending heavily on image-oriented advertising, but they are also contributing to the overall cost of doing business. You probably think that these products are more than the rest. However, the truth is, they are not as important as the name and image of the products they sell.

## *Search Carefully Online*

Due to various reasons, online shopping has become a preferred mode of shopping. It is a reasonably fast and convenient way to shop for multiple products and services. I sometimes prefer shopping online because it allows me to shop for products that I already want and get them delivered to me in a short amount of time. Thus, it saves time, effort and helps avoid getting stuck in traffic.

Despite the convenience and accessibility, some things can go wrong with shopping online. However, some things are worth avoiding. These are the potential downsides to shopping online and what you can and can't do about each of them:

- **Watch for hidden costs.** You can't go by the price of a product as advertised on websites. Websites that sell less expensive products may not be able to justify their fees. You may also be surprised at how much it costs to ship a product. Usually, the shipping cost is not disclosed until after you have finished your online purchase. So be wise before you click the button.
- **Understand that online shopping sometimes encourages overspending.** Online shopping encourages overspending. Not only do people tend to make purchases without using real cash, but they also tend to feel cheated when they complete their transactions. In addition, the link between social media and online shopping is very much intertwined with many sites.

Therefore, it can result in higher advertising and spending problems.

- **Beware of identity theft.** Not only are websites not secure, but they also tend to trick users into revealing their personal and financial details. Don't disclose your banking details to unknown and suspicious websites. This topic is a must-know for all of us, or else your bank account might be compromised.
- **Closely consider online reviews.** Some online reviews are biased, and some are bogus. Be wary of these types of reviews as they can lead to bad decisions. Be careful and suspicious when reading online reviews. There are quite a lot of means to find out if the reviews are authentic or not. The more the reviews, the more reliable it is. Or you may use the fakespot. com site.
- **Watch for counterfeit products and unauthorized retailers.** For example, if you shop for the best prices on a specific product online, you'll likely be led to sites selling fake merchandise. Even if the product is labeled as the real thing, the maker may not stand behind it in the way it usually would. So be sure to buy on Legit E-commerce platforms.

## *Get Rid of Additional Fees from Your Spending*

If you save money, you can cut down on all your expenses by *Ten* (10%) percent. You can reach your goal by varying the categories you cut or increase your income by creating multiple sources. For example, what you buy may be a habit rather than a specific purchase. In most cases, people tend to spend their money on something they really want or value.

Buying in bulk is a way to minimize costs. It saves you money on both the packaging and handling of the goods. However, what you spend is often a matter of habit rather than a definite need or value. So take the big picture in buying.

If you're a single person, shop with a friend and divide the bulk purchases into smaller portions. This will not just give you a wider choice but also allow you to save money. Even though it's unlikely to trim down costs, buying in bulk can still save you money. Some stores sell larger packages or lower prices for bulk purchases.

## Boost Your Savings through Budgeting

A budget is important in your successful financial planning.[26] Most people tend to think of budgeting as an unpleasant thought. It is hard to get-used to, especially when it comes to saving money. But, it can help you manage your spending and make it a habit.

Shop with a friend or partner and divide the bulk purchases into smaller batches if you're a single person. Most people think of budgeting as unpleasant thoughts. But, it can help you manage your money better.

The initial step in planning for your future spending is to analyze where your current money is going. Then, figure out how much more you would like to save each month. To get to your saving goals, you need to minimize unnecessary spending. First, make your cuts in areas that are least painful to you. Then, add up all of the savings you want to save to reach your goal.

Another method of budget planning is to start from scratch. Instead of just looking at your current expenses, start by asking yourself how much you want to spend on various categories. This method will let you see actually how much you should be spending.

Consider the following in making a budget:

- **Set up your financial goals.** Your financial direction is dependent on your financial plans. Planning is the foundation of your financial success. Take note of the saying, *If you fail to plan, you plan to fail.* Your financial goals are composed of your spending, saving, and investing plans. They should be specific, measurable, attainable, realistic, and time-based (S.M.A.R.T).

---

[26] A **budget** is a spending plan. It is the basis for effective money management. (Garman & Forgue, 2018. Personal Finance, Thirteenth Edition, Cengage Learning, pg. 92); (Kapoor et. Al, 2019. Personal Finance: An active Approach to Help you Achieve Financial Literacy, McGraw Hill Education, pg. 46).

- **Estimate all expected income from all sources.** After setting your goals, you have to estimate the available income for you. In consolidating your available income, include only the money that you are sure to receive. Estimate your income conservatively to avoid overspending.
- **Set amount for an emergency fund, current expenses, and long-term goals.** You have to anticipate unexpected expenses. The amount may vary depending on your needs and life situation. You also have to set aside your emergency fund and your financial goals. Avoid saving or allocating the amount left after your personal expenses. Often if you do this, there will be nothing left to save. Always remember the *pay yourself first* rule.
- **Set amounts for the things you are obliged to pay.** Remember that being responsible will keep you at ease with your financial matters. You have to take note of your priorities and monitor them based on their payment schedule and urgency.
- **Set amounts for your day-to-day living expenses.** Your daily expenses fluctuate depending on your life situation and needs. You may base your estimate on your past spending and the possible changes in your cost of living. Make sure that you don't sacrifice your needs over your wants.
- **Record your actual cash inflows and outflows.** It is important to record and compare your actual inflows and outflows. This will determine if you have established your spending plan well because there were cases where the actual spending plan was not the same as planned. In this case, you may either have a surplus or deficit. If you have an excess, then you can reallocate such in your savings. To avoid a deficit, always be conservative about your spending.
- **Keep tracking your saving and spending patterns periodically.** Take note that budgeting is a continuous process. Therefore, you need to review your spending plan regularly to know if you have to revise or adjust. This will also give you a review of your financial progress.

## Structure Your Emergency Funds

Preparing for the unexpected is a wise financial move. Even if you find *One Thousand* (₱1000) bills on the streets, you can't control the world around you. Generally, people should put away six months' worth of living expenses for emergencies.

In creating an emergency fund, you may want to ask this question: *How much emergency savings do I need depends on my situation?* To answer, check out the following:

- **Three months' living expenses:** Save up to three months' living expenses. It gives you savings and a lot of time. It also helps you maximize your investment options. This strategy works for people who are trying to maximize their investments elsewhere. It can also help them manage their expenses and build a stable income stream.
- **Six months' living expenses:** Six months' living expenses are typically enough to cover your basic living expenses. It is also appropriate if you have a low income or unstable job or career.
- **Up to one year's living expenses:** Reserve at least a year's living expenses in case your source of income fluctuates wildly from one year to the next.

If your only source of emergency funds is a credit card, then save at least three months' worth of living expenses before opening a retirement account or contributing to a savings account.

## Minimize Unnecessary Spending

Some strategies might work for you, and some won't. To start your budget reduction plan, start by choosing the right approach that works for you.

Work through them and find the one that works for you. Then, list down the options that are harder to achieve and those that may require more sacrifice.

This chapter will teach you how to implement a budget reduction strategy that will help you save money to invest and live comfortably in the future.

## Food Costs Management

Not eating is a poor long-term strategy for reducing food expenditures. However, it can be done in various ways to improve your health, not by starving yourself.

## Smart Dining

When saving money, eating out can be luxurious but can rack up big bills. In addition, some people hate to cook and don't have the time or energy to do it. This makes it difficult to order from the menu and enjoy the food.

Here are some tips for eating out:

- **Minimize beverages, especially alcohol.** Alcohol and soft drinks are big moneymakers for restaurants. They are delicious yet costly. It is not wrong to try them but instead of buying them, try bringing your tumbler with water. Water is good for the health and can bring a lot of benefits to the body and mind.
- **Consider buying prepared food and taking it home or eating it outside someplace lovely.** Buying prepared food instead of taking out at the grocery store can save you a lot of money. It saves you time and helps you prepare something that's already cooked. But nothing beats a home-cooked meal. It literally satisfies the body and soul.
- **Order vegetarian.** Since vegetarian dishes are cheaper than meat-based ones, they are a better alternative to expensive dinner entrees. But, again, I don't want to be a killjoy. For example, if you want to have dessert, try not to eat it with every meal. It will not just benefit your pocket but also your health.

## Home-cooked Meal at its Best

If you aren't skilled enough in the kitchen, try taking a cooking class or reading cook books. Having someone else teach you how to cook will teach you the basics. Even if you don't have formal cooking skills, it is still important that you keep a good inventory of the food that you like and that is reasonably priced. When shopping, make sure to buy enough to last for a couple of weeks.

The increasing popularity of weight loss and diet books has made most people eat better. In addition, they are purchasing organic and natural food in grocery stores. Although organic food is good for your health, it can also be costly. The key to being healthy and budget-friendly is to shop around and find deals at low prices.

Buying organic food makes sense when it comes to choosing fruits and vegetables. However, some of the most popular fruits and vegetables carry the most amount of pesticides. So select the not too much-infected one, which means it was not sprayed with pesticides nor treated with preservatives.

One area where many people waste money is in buying bottled water. While it is good for their health, most bottled water is not as pure as they think. If you're serious about saving money, install a water filtration system at home.

## Shelter Savings

According to Entrepreneur Robert Kiyosaki, a house is a liability if you are living in it.[27] After buying a house, several costs will be incurred to maintain it. However, it becomes an asset if you rent it out. Renting it out means that you have a cash inflow every month. Suppose you intend to live in the house. In that case, the other costs associated with

---

[27] According to **Robert Kiyosaki**, the rich people acquire assets, while the poor and middle class acquire liabilities. In addition, Real estate is one of the best investments you can make. He used his milestone success in real estate to find even more success. He leveraged his real estate success until his education company was lifted up and created more of it.

homeownership can consume a large portion of your monthly income. However, there are specific ways to save money on these expenses.

### Reduce Your Rental Fees

It is common for people to underestimate the amount of rent they pay each month. It can put away a large portion of your monthly take-home pay. If you think that rent is part of your expenses, here are some ways to cut it down:

- **Transfer to a lower-cost rental.** Looking for a lower-cost rental can be challenging, but it can also be a lifesaver. It can be located in a less popular and less congested area. Rent is more expensive in the commercialized area. On the other hand, renting a larger place with roommates is a great way to save money if you're in a sharing mood.
- **Purchase rather than rent if you can.** Although it's a luxury, living in a single home is also a good deal for your financial stability. It is also fulfilling, especially if you have passive income streams to maintain it. In addition, buying your house will save you from paying monthly rentals plus other costs.

### Treating Responsibly in Fun and Recreation

Having fun and enjoying time out for recreation can be well spent. Still, financial extravagance can ruin a reasonable budget. If you're not sure how much for entertainment you should spend, try taking advantage of some of the discounts offered by various attractions. Cultivate some low-cost or free activities that will improve your health and financial well-being.

### Enjoying while Spending Less on Vacations

Regardless of how you define vacations, remember that they aren't investments and should be financed through credit cards. But before you do that, you must have other contingencies like multiple sources of income.

If you're planning on traveling for a long time, consider taking advantage of the off-season deals on airfares and hotels accommodations. Several websites and magazines can help you find low-cost options. But, in some instances, even though a travel agent may be able to find you the best deal, they may not be able to find you the best prices.

## Be Wise with Gifts

How you approach gifts throughout the year can affect how much you spend on them. If you're planning on buying gifts for the holidays, think about how you will pay off those debts before the season ends. It is also important to avoid buying gifts that are too expensive.

Some people avoid giving gifts because they think that they are too cheap. However, paying attention to where and what you buy can save a lot of money.

Although I don't want to deny gifts, spend wisely. Homemade gifts are more affordable and may be more meaningful to the recipients.

# Part 3
## Building Wealth through Investing

Master fascinating concepts such as major types of investments, expected returns, risks, and diversification.

Explore the specific types of investments to choose from.

Master the fundamentals of investing in Stocks, Bonds, Forex, Cryptocurrencies, Real estate, and Businesses.

Protecting yourself, your family, and what you own through Insurance.

# Chapter 7
# Invest Your Time and Money Wisely

---

*It's not how much money you make, but how much money you keep,*
*how hard it works for you, and how many generations you keep it for.*
— *Robert Kiyosaki*

---

Getting started with making wise investments doesn't have to be complex. However, it can be very time-consuming and challenging to manage all of the many options out there. Consider time to explore the various issues that can affect your investment plan.

## *Build Your Goals*

Before investing, start planning for your goals and needs. Having goals help determine how long to invest the money and what to do with it. Also, it helps determine which strategies will work for you.

The level of risk that you should take into account when investing is relative to your comfort level and time frame. For example, high-risk vehicles can be dangerous if you don't have a lot of money to spend and are prone to suffering from stress.

You can not afford to take on too much risk with a down payment on a house because you will need it sooner or later.

You might be saving for a long-term goal, such as business. This means that you're in a better position to make risky investments than those designed to protect against losses.

If you're not sure about anything, consider investing in the stock market that's designed to give you time to prepare for the long-term. You can tolerate volatility, though it is not as easy as you think.

## Understanding the Primary Investments

For a moment, forget all the jargon and product names that have been thrown around in the investing world. Instead, focus on what an investment really is and how it can be done properly.

Imagine a world where there are only two investment flavors: chocolate and vanilla ice cream. The investment universe is just simple if you understand it. It is just a matter of supply and demand. Choose the supply side. Consider these investment choices: becoming a lender, a producer, or an owner.

The threat of inflation is that it grinds down the real savings and returns that most investors aim for.[28] This goal is at risk if the returns on investments are not kept up with the inflation rate. For instance, if an investment return is *Two percent (2%)* in a *Three percent (3%)* inflation environment, it will generate a negative return of *One perent (1%)*.

If investors do not protect themselves against inflation, their fixed income returns could be affected. Again, this is because they tend to buy securities that provide a stable income stream.

Since the interest rate on most fixed income instruments remains the same until they mature, the purchasing power declines as inflation rises.

Instead of diversifying their investments, some people tend to think that they can get a better rate of return by investing in a variety of bonds and Certificates of Deposit (CD). For instance, you want to beat inflation. In that case, your investment's rate of return shall be greater than the rate of reduction in purchasing power due to inflation.

---

[28] **Inflation,** is a rise in the general level prices. It reduces the value of a currency's purchasing power, having the effect of an increase in prices. It is computed as, **Percent inflation rate** = *(Final CPI Index Value/Initial CPI Value) x 100.* **Consumer Price Index (CPI),** measures the changes in the prices of goods and services purchased for consumption. (Garman & Forgue, 2018. Personal Finance, Thirteenth Edition, Cengage Learning, pg. 10); (Kapoor et. Al, 2019. Personal Finance: An active Approach to Help you Achieve Financial Literacy, McGraw Hill Education, pg. 6).

## Understanding Investment Returns

You may not share in the company's success where you borrow money from if its size and profits grow significantly. Your interest rate and principal will stay the same if this is the case.

During the past century, ownership investments have returned higher, significantly beating other investments such as bonds and savings accounts.

**TABLE 7.1 ROI of Different Investment Vehicles** [29]

| Rate of Return on ₱1,000 Invested | How Much in 25 Years | How Much in 40 Years |
|---|---|---|
| 4% (savings account) | ₱2,665.84 | ₱4,801.02 |
| 5% (bond) | ₱3,386.35 | ₱7,039.99 |
| 9% (stocks and real estate) | ₱8,623.08 | ₱31,409.42 |

You can't beat the market average returns if you keep your money on the sidelines. So if you want to harvest the benefits of investing, don't chase the latest investment after trying to beat the market average.

You can't earn good returns from stocks and real estate if you are stuck in cash. So instead, try to chase the market average returns and invest in them and other investment vehicles.

## Anticipate Investment Risks

Most people were not taught about what risk really means. For instance, a savings account might seem like a less risky option compared to the stock market. But there are greater risks if you just place your money in the bank, like Inflation risk and Interest rate risks.

In the long term, the stock market generally beats the inflation rate. In contrast, the interest rates on savings accounts are lower. So if you're planning on saving for a long-term goal, such as retirement, then your money should be invested and then placed on a savings account.

---

[29] https://www.calculator.net/investment-calculator.html

Before investing, take note of the following:

- What are my saving and investing goals?
- How long will I hold such an investment?
- What is my risk tolerance?
- Does my risk tolerance fit my investment appetite and the length of such investment?

Take these steps before you invest:

1. **Create your emergency fund.** If you have your emergency fund, your emotion will not be distorted due to a minimal loss. Without any backup, you tend to sell all your positions because you are afraid to be defeated.
2. **Do your research before investing.** Be a good investor. You have to understand your investment, the pros, and the cons. Remember that in investing, there is always risk. The bigger the risk, the bigger the return.
3. **Begin investing little money.** If you have the big capital and you are willing to risk it all, why not? But if you are still on level one, begin one step at a time. Master the art of reinvesting. There is no problem with increasing your investments.
4. **Never stop learning.** If you start investing, it is important to master it. Master the basics. Learn from the experts. Nurture your skills and develop strategies that best suit you.

## Level of risk of each investment vehicle[30]

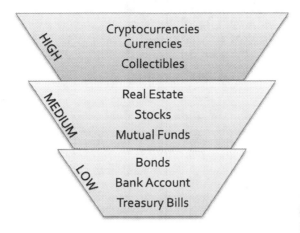

Before you start saving, I suggest that you first understand the types of appropriate investments for your goals and timeline. Then, determine the risk and rewards of your investing activities.

## Stocks and Bonds

Since real estate and stocks have higher historical returns, some people believe they should put all their money into these two investments. However, the risk with owning stocks and real-estate investments is that their value can fluctuate wildly in short-term periods.

If you want to be a value-investor like Warren Buffet, you should be patient with your investment. Think long-term, and don't rush. Remember that time mitigates risks. Holding a particular stock for a shorter period tends to be riskier than holding it in a longer period. However, having it for a long-term period is fair provided that such stock is growing in value. Growing in value means that even if the stock might experience short-term ups or downs, the important thing is that it is on the uptrend.

---

[30] **Typical Investments for Financial Security, Safety and Income, Growth and Speculation.** (Kapoor et. Al, 2019. Personal Finance: An active Approach to Help you Achieve Financial Literacy, McGraw Hill Education, pg. 356-358); (https://yourmoney. lumio-app.com/types-of-investments-and-their-risks/)

You should not invest all of your money in the stock or real estate market, rather, you should diversify. Having multiple sources of income is rewarding. It is a good idea to start investing in such volatile investments if you already have knowledge about the different markets. If not yet, then it will be too risky for you. If you are good at trading, that could be better, but yet, be careful.

The shorter time horizon between investing in stocks and bonds means that these investments are more likely to perform well than bonds.

Some types of bonds have higher-yielding characteristics, but the risk-reward ratio remains intact. If you plan on investing in the stock market, try practicing in different virtual platforms like Investagrams and others. For Bond investing, you may inquire in various banks or visit https://www.treasury.gov.ph.

## Risk Management Measures

Before starting a semester, I always asked my students about their expectations and what they would like to learn in my personal finance class. One of them said she wanted to learn to invest her money in the stock market while undervalued and then accumulate wealth.

She understood that there are risks to investing in stocks and becoming wealthy. She also believed that people could anticipate what the future holds. How did she get so excited about the stock market when it was undervalued? Of course, because of the internet. Everything is accessible on the internet nowadays. From reading materials, blogs, vlogs, podcasts, and other related information from various platforms.

Although investing in stocks and other high-growth investments can indeed be very volatile, there are various ways to reduce your risk.

Diversification is a strategy that can help minimize the risk of investing in certain vehicles. Invest in two to three stocks that you can monitor, don't rely on just one unless you have a good conviction. Don't put all your tomatoes in one basket because if one is damaged, all of them will come next.

Risk management is the most critical part of any investing activity. It is the balancing mechanism of decision-making. So even in doing business, it should be one of the things that are taken care of.

## Finding Low-risk, High-return Investments

Despite the credentials of many Master in Business Administration (MBA) professors, there are still low-risk investments that can provide promising returns.

If you're paying more than *Ten prcent* (10%) interest on a consumer loan, pay it off before investing. Doing so will give you a better return than taking out a loan and paying it off.

If you only have a limited months' worth of living expenses and cannot pay off debts, tapping into your emergency reserves may involve some risk. But, be sure to ask for backup sources if possible.

- **Your health is your best investment.** So relax, exercise, and maintain a balanced diet. Health is wealth.
- **Invest in your family and friends.** Your relationship with them is also important. It's happier to enjoy your wealth with them.
- **Invest in yourself.** Your growth should be one of your priorities. You can improve your personal and career development by taking advantage of various opportunities. If you don't know what's next, try taking on a new hobby or improving your communication skills. Or read books that might help you improve your mindset and skills.

If your risk tolerance is low and new to investing, here are some low-risk investments:

- **PAG-IBIG MP2.** This is a saving program for Filipino members of PAG-IBIG (Pagtutulungan sa Kinabukasan: Ikaw, Bangko, Industria at Gobyerno) who want to appreciate their funds. It is a tax-free, low-risk investment because it is held by the government. You can start at*Five Hundred* (₱500.00) and can earn up to *Six percent to Seven Percent* (6%-7%) returns annually.

After *Five* (5) years of maturity, you may withdraw the amount you invested.[31]

- **Time Deposit Account.** This is a safe way to secure your money. Aside from that, it is also insured by *Philippine Deposit Insurance Corporation* (PDIC). In addition, this is one way of putting your money in a bank as an investor with time-rate interest. This means that the interest depends on how long you will put your money in the bank. You may start at *One Thousand* (₱1000.00) and up. The thing is that there is a lock-in period where you can not withdraw the fund for the period you invested it.[32]

- **Government Bonds.** These are bonds issued by the government. Aside from it being one of the safest investments you could have, it is also tax-free. Retail Treasury Bonds (RTBs) are Low risk, fixed-term investments issued by the Republic of the Philippines through the Bureau of the Treasury to help you invest in a better future. It earns a fixed interest rate over the term up to 2.375% p.a. Interest payments are made quarterly for up to *Three* (3) years of maturity.[33]

## Investments Diversification

Diversification is a process where you place your money in various investments with varying returns. This means that when some of your assets are down in value, the other investment will probably increase. This concept helps minimize risk and maximize returns.[34]

---

[31] See the website for more info. https://www.pagibigfund.gov.ph/Membership_ Modified PagIBIG2.html

[32] **Time deposits** are fund deposits in a savings acoount. (Garman & Forgue, 2018. Personal Finance, Thirteenth Edition, Cengage Learning, pg. 161); (https://grit.ph/ time-deposit/)

[33] **Treasuries** are issued by any government. They are also known as Treasury Bills, Treasury Notes and Treasury Bonds. (Garman & Forgue, 2018. Personal Finance, Thirteenth Edition, Cengage Learning, pg. 161); (https://www.treasury.gov.ph/?page_ id=10532)

[34] **Diversification** is a technique that reduces risk by allocating investments across various financial instruments, industries, and other categories. (https://www. investopedia. com/ terms/d/diversification.asp)

To minimize the risk of all your investments going down simultaneously, you should put aside different types of investments. This includes stocks, bonds, and real estate.

Although it is important to invest in stocks, diversifying your portfolio can be very useful if you're looking for a broad-based return. Mutual funds and exchange-traded funds are both highly useful investment vehicles.

Take a look at the benefits of diversification:

- Diversification lets you achieve the same rate of return as a single investment.
- Diversification lets you obtain a higher rate of return for a given level of risk.

Even if you insist that you are the best, or your credentials are quite remarkable, there's a chance that your investment could lose money. However, having the proper diversification and risk management techniques can help you reduce risk and get rewarded.

## Asset Allocation: Creating Wealth

Asset allocation is the method of selecting the appropriate mix of investments for you. It involves carefully analyzing all of the various options available to you. Therefore, before you decide, it's important to consider all of the factors related to your financial situation.[35]

Money-market and short-term bond funds are good places to save for emergencies. Having a reserve of money that's accessible in an emergency is a good idea.

---

[35] **Asset allocation** is an investment strategy that aims to balance risk and reward by apportioning a portfolio's assets according to an individual's goals, risk tolerance, and investment horizon. It is the process of spreading your assets among several types of investment to lessen risk. (Garman & Forgue, 2018. Personal Finance, Thirteenth Edition, Cengage Learning, pg. 412-415); (Kapoor et. Al, 2019. Personal Finance: An active Approach to Help you Achieve Financial Literacy, McGraw Hill Education, pg. 356). (https://www.investopedia.com/terms/a/ assetallocation.asp)

Bonds can also be used for long-term investing. For instance, putting a portion of your money in bonds can help buffer market declines.

**TABLE 7.2 Allocating Your Long-Term Fund**

| Your Investment Age & Attitude | Bond Allocation (%) | Stock Allocation (%) |
|---|---|---|
| 20-30 yrs old (Aggressive) | 10-20% | 80-90% |
| 30-50 yrs old (Conservative) | 20-30% | 70-80% |
| 50 yrs old & up (Play-safe) | 50-80% | 20-50% |

Most people have a long-term goal in mind when it comes to investing their money for retirement. However, your age and the years until retirement are the biggest factors that will affect how much money you should put aside for the future.

One helpful guideline is dividing or allocating your money between long-term growth investments such as stocks and more conservative ones such as bonds.

If you are 30 years old, you start investing in stocks at *Eighty percent* (80%) and gradually increase your total investment to *Ninety percent* (90%) over the years. On the other hand, if you're a conventional investor who doesn't want a lot of risks but still values the importance of striving for growth, you may be a conservative type.

Suppose the 40-year-old investor has a total of *Seventy percent* (70%) invested in stocks. In that case, he can easily invest up to *Thirty Five percent* (35%) in international stock funds and the other *Thirty Five percent* (35%) in domestic stock funds, and *Thirty percent* (30%) in bonds.

If you're a play-safe investor, consider allocating a portion of your fund's assets to overseas investments and a greater percentage for bonds since it is safer.

## *Hold Your Allocations: Don't Trade*

If you are not yet a skilled trader, make time to study and master being one. If you intend to invest long-term, don't trade. Your risk appetite should drive the allocation of your assets. As you get older, gradually reducing your riskiness should make sense.

Don't tinker with your portfolio daily or weekly. Instead, it is important to keep track of your portfolio's mix each year or so to get the most out of it.

Instead of trading blindly, avoid engaging in strategies that are designed to produce below-average returns. This strategy provides short-term comfort, but it can also make below-average returns in the long run.

When an investment gets featured in a news story, it's time to take a deep breath and ask yourself if it is really worth the hype. Instead, it may be headed for a downward trend.

Many people want to buy everything from clothes to cars on sale. However, when the market is booming, most investors are quick to exit without even trying to make a great buy.

## International Stocks Investing

Aside from stocks in the Philippines, there are also stocks in other countries. For example, you can invest in U.S stocks or other countries. *Why would you want to invest in international stocks?*

Here are some reasons:

- Foreign stocks have excellent growth potential. If you look for the total value of all stocks globally, the value of foreign stocks exceeds that of PH stocks.
- While PH stocks are attractive, international investors can also benefit from the opportunities presented by the growing economies in other countries.
- When you only invest in PH stocks, you miss out on the opportunities available to investors in other countries.

Some people are reluctant to invest in overseas stocks due to concerns that their actions could hurt the country or contribute to a loss of Pinoy jobs. Second, they are only focused on one index, not knowing that they can profit from the growth of foreign economies.

In fact, we already live in a global economy where all countries are linked economically. Opportunities to earn and build wealth are everywhere. Take action.

So, where are the significant investing opportunities outside the Country? International investing managers generally look at opportunities in three major geographic regions: [36]

- Latin America: Includes countries such as Argentina, Brazil, Chile, Columbia, Costa Rica, Mexico, Panama, and Peru.
- Europe: Includes countries such as Belgium, Denmark, France, Germany, Ireland, Italy, Netherlands, Norway, Spain, Sweden, Switzerland, and the United Kingdom.
- Asia-Pacific: Includes countries such as Australia, China, India, Japan, Hong Kong, India, New Zealand, Singapore, South Korea, Taiwan, Thailand, and Vietnam.

Another way foreign stocks are categorized is between developed markets, emerging markets, and Frontier Markets.

Developed markets are characterized by more mature, stable, and secure economies with relatively high living standards. Examples include Australia, Canada, France, Germany, Japan, Switzerland, and the United Kingdom.[37]

Emerging markets are more volatile and typically higher growth economies in their early economic stages. Examples include Brazil,

---

[36] (A)https://www.thoughtco.com/official-listing-of-countries-world-region-1435153
   (B)https://openknowledge.worldbank.org/handle/10986/18843?show=full
   (C)https://www.investopedia.com/terms/g/geographical-diversification.asp
[37] https://www.nasdaq.com/articles/what-difference-between-developed-emerging-and-frontier-market-2012-05-11

China, Chile, India, Indonesia, Malaysia, Mexico, Russia, South Africa, and Thailand.[38]

Frontier markets are a subset of the emerging market category. It means that they are also emerging markets, but not all of them are included. Examples are Colombia, Indonesia, Vietnam, Egypt, Turkey, South Africa, Nigeria, Bangladesh, and Botswana.[39]

Suppose you want to start investing in the international stock market. In that case, you may try global trading platforms like Etoro and others.

## Creating Wealth with Real Estate

Since real estate has historically provided higher returns than stocks, it has been considered a time-tested method of wealth creation. However, like stocks, they can also go through ups and downs.

Most people make money investing in real estate by doing their due diligence before they buy. They usually invest for many years and do their homework to ensure they get the best deal possible. When choosing real estate for investment, remember that the fuel for housing demand is local economic growth.

When exploring potential properties, run the numbers to determine the cash demands and profitability of owning a house.

Getting into real estate is a great way to build wealth and increase your net worth. The equity in your home can become a significant portion of your total assets. In addition, equity can be used to fund various goals, such as education, retirement, and buying a house. It is also less expensive than renting it.

---

[38] https://www.nasdaq.com/articles/what-difference-between-developed-emerging-and-frontier-market-2012-05-11

[39] https://www.nasdaq.com/articles/what-difference-between-developed-emerging-and-frontier-market-2012-05-11

Real estate is different from other investments. The following are reasons why real estate is unique:

- You can't live in stocks, bonds, or mutual funds. Real estate is an investment where you can live and generate income if rented or leased.
- It appreciates in value. The good thing about these lands and other properties is that they do not depreciate. The building may, but its land does not.
- Due to the limited supply of land and the demand for housing, the Earth's population continues to grow. Real-estate prices are so high that it is difficult to find new land to construct new homes in some populated areas.
- Zoning is a process that affects the value of a property. It helps determine what uses can be allowed for it. This strategy will help you reap the benefits of future real-estate values. It's also important to note that some properties may not have been developed to their full potential. This strategy will help you avoid making mistakes and maximize the value of your real estate investment.
- Unlike other investments, real estate is not prone to cash flow problems. In fact, it can be bought with a large amount of money, which is typically *Eighty percent to Ninety percent* (80%) to (90%) of the property's value. This method of borrowing is known as exercise leverage. However, real estate has its own drawbacks. Aside from being a costly investment, it can also suffer from frequent headaches as a landlord. But it pays in the long term.

Real estate is similar to other types of investments. However, it can be bought and sold differently depending on the area and the demand for properties. For example, you can invest in properties and then rent them out. This method works for investors who are looking for long-term capital gains.

Despite the advantages of real estate, it has its limitations. For instance, buying a house can be very costly. At the same time, it has low liquidity. It takes time to sell it. While it may seem like a simple task, being a landlord can be stressful sometimes. Conduct a cost-benefit analysis to weigh the positive and the negative.[40] Consider a few things when it comes to managing your rental property expenses.

## Real Estate Versus Stocks

Since real estate and stocks have both produced equal returns, you may end up with a better investment than you initially thought. However, before making a decision, consider these factors:

- The first question to ask yourself when it comes to becoming a landlord is; *Is it possible to handle the responsibilities of owning a rental property?*
- Although stocks can be very time-consuming, they can also be done through professionally managed mutual funds or exchange-traded funds.
- Since real estate investment is risky, many people avoid paying taxes while accumulating their down payment.
- Do you have a better understanding of real estate? If so, then it could be an excellent time to consider investing. Some people are uncomfortable with stocks and funds due to their perceived complexity. If you better understand what makes real estate tick, then it's a good investment.
- Some people enjoy the challenge of managing rental properties. In contrast, others are good at it and can make money doing it. When you are good at it, you can make money and enjoy every minute of it.

Real-estate investors get the pleasure of displaying their wealth in a way that others can only envy. This is not to say that they can't pick stocks, but they can't get the same pleasure from a portfolio that shows their wealth.

---

[40] **A cost-benefit analysis** is a systematic process that businesses use to analyze which decisions to make and which to forgo. (Garman & Forgue, 2018. Personal Finance, Thirteenth Edition, Cengage Learning, pg. 42); (https://www.investopedia.com/terms/c/cost-benefitanalysis.asp)

If you're unsure which type of investment to make, residential real estate may be an attractive option. However, it's a risky investment and will require more time and effort to monitor and manage. Real estate investment trusts are good ways to avoid the rental real estate market's many shortcomings.

Real estate investment trusts are often referred to as REITs. They are typically focused on one or two types of property. You can invest in REITs through various means, such as buying stocks in the major stock exchanges or a real-estate mutual fund.[41]

## Investing in Business and Your Career

Small business is the leading source of wealth creation. There are many ways to invest in one. You can start one yourself, buy an existing business, or invest in someone else's.

## Creating Your Own Enterprise

When you start a new venture, it is important to step into the shoes of someone who has already established a successful one. Consider what skills and expertise you have that can be used in your venture.

You don't need to be perfect or have a huge capital before starting one. You just need to start and learn through the process.

A written business plan is the first step to developing a plan for your idea. It should contain all the details of your business operation. It also includes the costs and the potential profitability of the venture.

---

[41] **Real Estate Investment Trust** (REIT) is a stock corporation established in accordance with the Corporation Code of the Philippines and the rules and regulations promulgated by the Securities and Exchange Commission (SEC) principally for the purpose of owning income-generating real estate assets. It is a special kind of closed-end investment company. (Garman & Forgue, 2018. Personal Finance, Thirteenth Edition, Cengage Learning, pg. 470); (https://ndvlaw.com/on-real-estate-investment-trust-reit-how-to-engage-in-a-reit-business -in-the-philippines/)

People build their own businesses because they want to work for their own. Nevertheless, it is usually harder to start a new business than working from a part-time job.

I wouldn't trade my experience running my own business for anything else. Although, admittedly, it's a bit challenging to build a stable one. Still, there are many reasons why people fail to succeed in starting a small business; one is of being negative.

If you have the time and passion, you can start a business and a job without much effort. However, if you don't do a good job marketing, your chances of succeeding are slim.

Before planning to start a business, think about the risks of not fulfilling your dreams. If you think about the risks of not fulfilling them, you may regret not taking the opportunity.

## Buy a Business

If you haven't figured out specific products or services that you want to sell but are good at running a business, owning one may be for you.

It takes a long time to find a good business, and it is important to start searching for one early to get a good idea of how long it will take. Although owning a small business doesn't require much capital, it does require specific skills and experience to successfully run it.

The history of the company and how it operates will tell you what kind of ownership you should have. Having a hard time making tough decisions and forcing people to change their ways is not ideal for you.

Some people believe that buying an existing business is safer than starting a new one. However, this is typically not the case. Sometimes, buying an existing business can be very risky.

If you can't run the business, then you may be forced to sell it. This can be a financial burden that can lead to bankruptcy. On the other hand, if the business is already successful, the current owner should be selling it for a premium to reflect its lack of risk.

## Invest in Someone else's Business

Are you a person who likes the idea of owning a small business but doesn't want the headaches of running it? Then, maybe you should consider investing in another person's business. Although this route may seem like it can be easily done, it can be challenging to follow.

Are you good at evaluating the financial statements of private companies? While it is common to invest in a private company, there are some differences to consider when doing so. Unlike public companies, private firms are not required to produce complete and accurate financial statements. This means that you are more prone to having an inaccurate financial report when evaluating a small firm.

Unlike large companies, private companies don't advertise their investment opportunities. Instead, they find potential investors by connecting with business advisors. You can also find exciting investment opportunities by speaking with individuals who are building small businesses.

If you can't afford to lose all of what is invested, don't consider investing in a private company. Ideally, you should have enough assets to invest in small, privately held companies. But, these should only represent a portion of your total financial assets.

## The New Path of Investment Probabilities

Sometimes, some investments belong to their own planet. This section will talk about the unusual investments that are not owned by a corporation or institution.

### Foreign Exchange

Foreign exchange can be a great way to expand your portfolio. Learning about the basics can help you start confidently and build a solid foundation for this asset class. However, it entails a bit of work to get started. This guide walks through all of the basics that you need to know to get started.

In foreign exchange, investors buy and sell the currencies of different countries.[42] This process is carried out through the foreign exchange market.

Each foreign exchange transaction involves the exchange of one currency for another. This process is known as pairs.

Foreign currencies are usually grouped in the following:

- **Major pairs:** These include the US Dollar (USD), the Euro (EUR), Japan yen (JPY), and British pound (GBP). This group is frequently traded.
- **Minor pairs:** These include various frequently traded currencies except the US Dollar.
- **Exotics:** These are typically paired with a thinly traded one. For instance, the USD may be paired with the Singapore Dollar (SGD) or the Hong Kong Dollar (HKD).
- **Regional pairings:** Regional pairings are based on the same geographic region. For instance, European and Asian currencies can be exchanged for each other.

## *Investing in Currencies*

Foreign exchange trading is a type of investment that takes advantage on the fluctuations in the value of a given currency. It works by buying a particular currency and selling it at a profit.[43]

---

[42] **The foreign exchange market** (also known as forex, FX, or the currencies market) is an over-the-counter (OTC) global marketplace that determines the exchange rate for currencies around the world.Currency trading is volatile and uses a lot of margin which is risky. (Garman & Forgue, 2018. Personal Finance, Thirteenth Edition, Cengage Learning, pg. 510); (https://www. investopedia.com/terms/forex/f/foreign-exchange-markets.asp)

[43] **Currency trading** is buying or selling currency pairs in the foreign exchange market at a specific exchange rate. (https://www.thebalance.com/what-is-currency-trading-1344894)

You may also want to consider how they are ordered. For example, if you pair USD with GBP, the base currency is called USD, and the quote currency is called GBP.

A mutual fund or stocks can be traded on a central exchange, such as the PSE, NYSE, etc. On the other hand, instead of going through a bank, Forex goes through the foreign exchange market.

Trading in the Forex is done through a brokerage firm. Here are several ways you can trade currency:

- **Spot trading.** It is an alternative form of currency trading. It is similar to an exchange where the price of a pair is determined when the trade is settled.
- **Forward trading.** You can trade foreign exchange forwards with a set price that will be settled in the future. This provides you peace of mind and reduces volatility.
- **Future trading.** It is similar to forward trading. The only difference is that it involves entering into a contract based on the exchange rate of a certain currency. The price is determined by the foreign exchange rate.

You can buy or sell a pair depending on the exchange rate. If you decide to buy a pair, the base currency will increase in value. If you choose to sell, the base currency will decline in value.

Currency Investing can give several advantages:

- **Accessibile and Convenient.** The stock markets operate during set hours. This means that you can only trade in the market before or after the scheduled closing hours. While Forex Trades can be made any time of the day and night.
- **Diversified.** Diversification can help manage risk. For example, foreign exchange can help minimize volatility.
- **Low costs.** Compared to stocks, foreign currencies have lower commissions. This means that you can hold on to more of your returns.

Aside from these advantages, there is one main disadvantage to currency investing:

- **Volatility.** The risks associated with foreign exchange trading are higher than those associated with other investment strategies. Therefore, it is wise to consider your risk tolerance before taking on this exciting new venture.

Understanding the ins and outs of investing in foreign currencies can be challenging, most likely if your first time. However, this helps you make well-versed decisions when it comes to making currency purchases.

If you're not comfortable with the complex foreign exchange market, consider investing in exchange-traded funds (ETF). These funds are more tax-efficient and are typically more active.[44]

## Valuable Metals

Gold and silver were being used as a medium of exchange for thousands of years. As a result, their value has been based on scarcity[45]

With the rise of paper money, the government can now print more. This process can result in the deflation of a currency and inflation. A rise in inflation can be considered a hedge against it. During the 1970s and 1980s, the rise in inflation depressed bonds and stocks.

---

[44] **An Exchange Traded Fund** (ETF) is a cross between a stock and a mutual fund. It is like a mutual funds (MF) or a unit investment trust fund. It is an investment company that buy equities or shares of companies like PLDT, Jollibee, Aboitiz, SM, Ayala, etc. (Garman & Forgue, 2018. Personal Finance, Thirteenth Edition, Cengage Learning, pg. 469); (https://pesolab.com/etf-exchange-traded-fund/)

[45] **Gold** is a uniquely private, personal way to hold some genuine wealth. (Garman & Forgue, 2018. Personal Finance, Thirteenth Edition, Cengage Learning, pg. 508); (https://www.forbes.com/sites/nathanlewis/2015/12/26/the-history-of-gold-is-really-the-history-of-the-goldsilver-complex/

From 1972 to 1980, gold and silver rose significantly in value. However, after reaching their peak in 2011, the prices of these metals declined significantly.[46]

Beating inflation is by hedging. You invest in precious metals through mutual funds or exchange-traded funds. Gold and silver futures are not investments. Instead, they are short-term gambles on which way the prices will move. So before you acquire them, make sure to avoid getting ripped-off.

Here are some benefits of investing in valuable metals:

- **Stability:** Since gold prices do not fluctuate much during a crisis, it is more advantageous to invest in gold than stocks. Its steady growth and low volatility make it an attractive investment option for investors.
- **Easy to buy:** You can easily buy gold from a jeweler if you have the required capital. However, it is important to buy gold that has purity.
- **Inflation reaper:** Gold has historically performed well against inflation. It can also outperform fixed deposits during economic highs and lows. The value of a currency goes down when the economy goes down. This means that gold is a great way to hedge against inflation.
- **Steady Growth:** Although gold is a finite metal, its value can still rise over the long term. Its volatility can be unpredictable.
- **Good Collateral:** Gold can be used as a security for loans. This benefit is usually applicable to emergency situations.

Though it is a good investment, it comes with few limitations:

- **Security Issues:** Physical gold assets are usually prone to theft. In contrast, digital gold can be secure and easily accessed by investors.

---

[46] Gold prices were stagnant, then soared and crashed again. (Garman & Forgue, 2018. Personal Finance, Thirteenth Edition, Cengage Learning, pg. 508); (https://www.businessinsider.com/todays-gold-market-looks-a-lot-like-the-crazy-1970s-2016-7)

- **High Fees:** Gold may be an easy purchase, but it comes with various commissions. While it is fine to buy gold, it is also a risky purchase due to its commissions. Gold ETFs are more advantageous because you can buy and sell gold bullion without paying the charges. If you want to invest without paying the fees, then there are various options available.
- **Purity Issues:** The actual value of gold depends on its purity. Its purity is measured by the karat value. This is an issue when you want to own physical gold. But this will not matter if you invest in the digital market.

Physical gold is a commodity that has certain risks, such as storage and theft. However, these risks are not present in gold mutual funds and gold ETFs.

## Bitcoin and other Cryptocurrencies

Perhaps you have heard of Bitcoin.[47] It is an online currency that works seamlessly through the Internet. Young adults tend to know more about it than older adults.

Every year, Bitcoin has become more popular. Unfortunately, it has had one of the most volatile trading records in all the asset classes. Its first price increase happened in 2010, and it has since gone through several rallies and crashes. In 2017, its price surpassed the $20,000 mark. Its price reached almost $24,000 in December 2020, a *Two Hundred Twenty Four percent* (224%) increase from the start of the year.[48]

The price movements of Bitcoin are influenced by both its promise and investor enthusiasm. Its creator Satoshi Nakamoto envisioned it

---

[47] Bitcoin, a cyber currency, also called cryptocurrency or virtual currency. This digital asset serves as a payment method using cryptography. (Kapoor et. Al, 2019. Personal Finance: An active Approach to Help you Achieve Financial Literacy, McGraw Hill Education, pg. 123)

[48] https://www.investopedia.com/articles/forex/121815/bitcoins-price-history.asp

to circumvent the banking infrastructure crisis after the 2008 financial collapse.[49]

Bitcoin is a marketing gimmick that is meant to sound like a real coin. But, unlike fiat money, it's not backed yet by any physical commodities or institution. Entrepreneur Wences Casares said that Bitcoin is not a currency for a government. It is a global currency for the people. [50]

Many people who have Bitcoin continue to hold onto them in hopes that its price will keep rising. Its promoters are expecting its price to keep increasing. Like Amazon.com and Apple, its promoters are expecting big price hikes. As a result, people don't hoard money as they did with stocks.

Ethereum is also a cryptocurrency that has gained popularity.[51] This is due to its ability to provide decentralized transactions and the use of smart contracts.

The previous price fluctuations were primarily caused by retail investors and speculators who could not explain the fluctuations of Bitcoin. However, this new narrative is large because various factors outside of retail investors influence Bitcoin's price.

Bitcoin looks attractive, but it comes with some risks. Here are some major issues:

- **No repercussions or recourse:** Bitcoin transactions are anonymous yet can be done without any option or outcomes. The nature of cryptocurrencies makes them attractive to

---

[49] **Satoshi Nakamoto** is the pseudonym who penned the original Bitcoin whitepaper and is the identity credited with inventing Bitcoin itself. (https://www.investopedia. com/ terms/s/satoshi-nakamoto.asp)

[50] **Wences Casares** is a technology entrepreneur with global business experience specializing in technology and financial ventures. He is Founder and Chief Executive Officer of Lemon Wallet. (https://www.weforum.org/people/wences-casares)

[51] **Ethereum** (ETH) is a cryptocurrency. It is scarce digital money that you can use on the internet – similar to Bitcoin. If you're new to crypto, here's how ETH is different from traditional money. (https://ethereum.org/en/eth/)

individuals involved in illegal activities because they cannot be traced.

- **No inherent value:** Contrast that with gold, which has a long history of being utilized as a medium of exchange. Also, gold is cheaper than Bitcoin due to its scarcity. Its price is determined by the amount of gold that's extracted from the ground.
- **Not unlimited:** Bitcoin is not unlimited. Its supply is artificially limited, and as more people start using it online, its value will eventually tumble.
- **Not yet universally accepted:** Despite Bitcoin's popularity, many merchants don't accept it yet. This is a common insult to the users, as unfavorable conversion rates are typically added to the price of an item bought with Bitcoin.

Bitcoin has virtually no intrinsic value as a digital currency. So if you pay thousands of dollars for it, you might end up disappointed.

With more than *Eleven Thousand Nine Hundred Fifty Two* (11,952) cryptocurrencies, the field is getting bigger.[52] Many creators are hoping to get into the ground floor of the next generation of digital currencies.

## The Future of Digital Currency

Bill Gates, the founder of Microsoft said that the future of money is a digital currency. [53]

In a global contest, governments of different countries are now engaged in digitalizing their currencies. This could create a new benchmark currency and disrupt financial transactions globally. It could create a new global standard for money.

Cash has been declining in use for years, as the convenience of electronic transactions has taken it. Money will be smart, but it will also be in danger of making wrong decisions if not fully regulated.

---

[52] https://coinmarketcap.com/all/views/all/
[53] https://www.marketwatch.com/story/bill-gates-says-cryptocurrency-is-one-innovation-the-world-could-do-without-11613662510

Rick Falkvinge, Founder of the Swedish Pirate Party said that Bitcoin might do to banks what email did to the postal industry.[54]

Before it became a speculative bubble, bitcoin was still in its beta stage because it could serve as a safe haven for people and businesses globally. Bitcoin was initially built to allow people to send and receive money without going through a third-party intermediary. However, its decentralized nature made it possible to do a wide range of previously impossible things.

Bitcoin is a cryptocurrency that offers a unique set of advantages when compared to other payment methods. Let's take a look at Bitcoin and its various benefits.

- **User Autonomy.** Unlike Bitcoin, fiat currencies are subject to various restrictions and risks. Because of this, many users might end up with bank runs and crashes. This is due to their lack of control over their money. However, it's not an issue in some cases since Bitcoin is not linked to any government policies.
- **Peer-to-peer Transactions basis.** Bitcoin is a mutual payment system. Its users can send and receive payments from anyone in the world. Unless they send or receive Bitcoin from a regulated institution, parties do not need approval from an external source.
- **No banking fees.** Bitcoin users are not subjected to the same fees that are typically associated with fiat currencies. Instead, they are not charged account maintenance fees, minimum balance fees, and no return deposit fees.
- **Low transaction fees for international payments.** Unlike other online payment systems, users of Bitcoin can pay for their coins wherever they have Internet access. This makes it possible for individuals to pay for goods and services without going to a physical store or bank.
- **Secured Transactions.** Bitcoin is not a physical currency. Its holder is the private key that is stored inside a wallet. This

---

[54] **Rick Falkvinge**, a Swedish information technology entrepreneur, Bitcoin advocate and founder of the Swedish Pirate Party. He is currently a political evangelist with the party, spreading the ideas across the world.

makes it hard for hackers to steal. Due to the nature of Bitcoin transactions, it is secure even though it is vulnerable to hacks.

- **Accessible to users.** Due to the nature of Bitcoin's decentralized network, users can send and receive Bitcoin without using a computer or a smartphone.

Despite the hype, the future of digital currency is still under development. Promoters see it as a way to make money, while critics believe it's a risky venture.

## Annuities

Annuities are investment products that are backed by insurance companies. They are usually accounts that pay a fixed interest rate. The rate that you receive is typically set one year ahead of time. However, it can vary depending on the returns that are provided by the investment.[55]

Unlike traditional retirement accounts, annuity contributions are tax-free until they are withdrawn.

Although an annuity can be a great way to save for retirement, it should only be considered after you have fully funded your tax-deductible retirement accounts.

## Collectibles

The collectible category includes various items such as art, jewelry, watches, and stamps. It also includes collectible items such as coins, art, and sports memorabilia. Or any material object that, through some kind of human manipulation, has become more valuable to certain humans.[56]

---

[55] https://businessmirror.com.ph/2019/07/24/annuities-as-retirement-income/

[56] **A collectible** refers to an item that is worth far more than it was originally sold for because of its rarity and/or popularity such as antiques, stamps, rare coins, art, paintings, etc. (Garman & Forgue, 2018. Personal Finance, Thirteenth Edition, Cengage Learning, pg. 507); (https://www.investopedia.com /terms/c/ collectible.asp)

Since long-term capital gains are taxed higher than ordinary income tax rates, they rarely keep up with inflation. Also, they are subject to markups that can add up quickly.

Treat collectible purchases as a hobby instead of an investment. Buy them with the hopes of making money instead of just being able to collect. Strictly avoid the markups and buy directly from the artist.

## *Mutual Funds and Exchange-Traded Funds*

Mutual funds and ETFs are among the best inventions of their kind. They are known for their success due to their various advantages.[57] Understanding the various advantages of investing in mutual funds and ETFs is very important. You may want to consider the following:

- **Professional management:** A portfolio manager and a research team manage mutual funds and exchange-traded funds. These funds and exchange-traded funds are managed by a team of professionals who thoroughly screen the universe of investments to find the best match for their stated objectives.

Fund managers typically attend the country's top business and finance schools to learn how to manage risk and make smart investing decisions. As a result, most of them have at least a decade of experience analyzing and selecting securities.

- **Low fees:** The most widely used stock mutual funds and exchange-traded funds typically have low costs. Because they buy and sell thousands of shares of a security, the percentage of commissions they generally pay is less than what you pay on your own. No-load funds are also known to avoid paying sales commissions.

---

[57] **A mutual fund** is a pool of money from the public that is invested with an expectation of a profit. Because of the way it invites people to invest, it is also called pooled or managed fund. (Garman & Forgue, 2018. Personal Finance, Thirteenth Edition, Cengage Learning, pg. 154); (https://pesolab.com/philippine-mutual-funds-for-beginners-how-to-start-investing/)

- **Diversification:** Fund investing allows you to achieve a level of a diversified portfolio that is difficult to reach without a lot of time and resources. Diversification is a process of achieving a level of risk management that can be difficult to achieve without a lot of time and resources.
- **Minimal cost of entry:** Most mutual funds have low minimum investment requirements. The low cost makes them attractive to people who have a lot of money and want to minimize their expenses.
- **Audited performance records and expenses:** Annual reports and other documents that detail fund performance is required by law to be filed with the SEC. Many firms also provide statistical data that can be used to evaluate a fund's performance.
- **Flexibility in risk level:** You can customize the level of risk that fits your goals and financial situation. If you're not comfortable with the volatility of stocks, you may want to consider funds that invest in bonds.

## Discovering Various Types of Fund

Fund names can be misleading. For instance, a stock fund may not be entirely invested in stocks, but a portion could be invested in bonds.

**Note:** If you haven't figured out the previous chapters that outline investing concepts, please read over again to understand the rest of the chapter.

## Money-market Funds

Money-market funds are considered the safer type of mutual funds for people worried about losing their money. Unlike bank savings accounts, they do not fluctuate.[58]

---

[58] **A money market fund** is a type of mutual fund that invests in cash and low-risk, short-term debt securities like treasury bills and commercial papers or short-term obligations issued by corporations. (Garman & Forgue, 2018. Personal Finance, Thirteenth Edition, Cengage Learning, pg. 471); (https://www.forbes.com/advisor/investing/what-is-money-market-fund/)

Money-market funds are very popular with individuals and institutions. These funds are often regulated by the SEC. General-purpose money-market funds invest in safe, short-term bank certificates of deposit, treasuries, and corporate commercial paper (short-term debt). It is issued by the largest and most creditworthy companies.

Money-market funds have been incredibly safe since they were first introduced during the 1970s.[59] Since they are very similar to bank accounts, their risk-free status makes them an excellent investment option for retail investors. However, these are only allowed to invest in securities with a maturity of fewer than *One Hundred Twenty* (120) days.

Money-market funds are typically not insured because they invest in securities backed by the government. As a result, this type of account is usually less risky than other types of accounts.

Explore the different types of funds from any banks or financial brokers.

## *Bond Funds*

A bond is an IOU[60] that is issued by a corporation or government agency. When you borrow money from a bond fund, it's typically a large group of bonds.

Bond funds typically invest in bonds that have the same maturity. The average length of their bonds generally is around five years.[61]

A short-term bond fund typically focuses on bonds that are due in the next two to three years. Conversely, a long-term fund tends to hold bonds that are expected to mature in over ten years.

---

[59] https://www.forbes.com/advisor/investing/what-is-money-market-fund/

[60] An IOU, a phonetic acronym of the words "I owe you," is a document that acknowledges the existence of a debt. (https://www.investopedia.com/terms/i/iou.asp)

[61] **A bond fund**, also referred to as a debt fund, is a pooled investment vehicle that invests primarily in bonds (government, municipal, corporate, convertible) and other debt instruments, such as mortgage-backed securities (MBS). (Kapoor et. Al, 2019. Personal Finance: An active Approach to Help you Achieve Financial Literacy, McGraw Hill Education, pg. 431); (https://www.investopedia.com/terms/b/bondfund.asp)

Instead of buying and holding bonds until they mature, a bond fund typically invests in new bonds to maintain its average maturity. This means that if you know that you will need a certain amount back on a certain date, you may want to consider buying individual bonds.

Bond funds are tax-free investments that can be used to invest in retirement accounts. They are usually suitable for people with a high tax bracket. In addition, bond funds are ideal for when you want to save for a rainy day or when you need to minimize risk.

Also, investing in bonds is a safer alternative to buying one individual bond. Also, it is cheaper than buying a single bond.

Most people can't easily determine the true value of bonds, leading to steep markups or markdowns. A more institutional investor can more easily avoid these types of markups.

## Stock Funds

Equity funds are typically focused on stocks. Thus, they are often referred to as *equity funds*.[62]

A stock is first defined by its size. The total market value of its outstanding shares is then computed. These stocks have high valuations relative to their current earnings and asset values. They typically pay low dividends.

- **Growth Stocks.** These stocks are characterized by high stock prices relative to their book values and rapid growth. However, since these companies tend to invest in their infrastructure, they typically pay low dividends.[63]

---

[62] **A Stock Fund,** also called equity fund is a mutual fund that invests principally in stocks. It can be actively or passively managed. (Kapoor et. Al, 2019. Personal Finance: An active Approach to Help you Achieve Financial Literacy, McGraw Hill Education, pg. 430); (https://www.investopedia.com/terms/e/equityfund.asp)

[63] **Growth Stocks,** Corporations that are leaders in their field. (Garman & Forgue, 2018. Personal Finance, Thirteenth Edition, Cengage Learning, pg. 428); (https://www. investopedia.com/ articles/professionals/072415/value-or-growth-stocks-which-best.asp)

- **Value Stocks.** A good value stock is one that investors look for. They want to own stocks that are cheap and have good growth potential.[64]

A mutual fund's investment philosophy is often defined by the type of stocks it selects. For example, a fund may choose to invest in large-company growth stocks or small-company value stocks.

## Hybrid Funds: Bonds and Stocks

Hybrid funds typically invest in a variety of securities. [65]They are less volatile and are usually less risky than funds that exclusively focus on stocks. During an economic recession, bonds tend to perform better than stocks.

A hybrid mutual fund is a type of fund that tries to maintain a consistent mix of investments in stocks and bonds. It does so by considering the portfolio manager's expectations for the duration of the investment cycle.

Most funds that shift money around are not very good at beating the market averages over a long period. They also tend to decrease their risk over time.

These funds are designed to appeal to people approaching a specific future goal, such as a child's college education or retirement.

Hybrid funds make investing simple. They provide investors with extensive diversification and lower volatility.

---

[64] **Value Stocks,** Companies that grow with the economy and tend to trade at a low price relative to its company fundamentals (dividends, earnings, sales and so on). Corporations that are leaders in their field. (Garman & Forgue, 2018. Personal Finance, Thirteenth Edition, Cengage Learning, pg. 428); (https://www.investopedia.com/articles/professionals/072415/value-or-growth-stocks-which-best.asp)

[65] **A Hybrid Fund** is an investment fund that is characterized by diversification among two or more asset classes. These funds typically invest in a mix of stocks and bonds. They may also be known as asset allocation funds. (https://www.investopedia.com/terms/h/hybridfund.asp)

## Index Funds

Index funds are funds that can be managed by a computer. They replicate an index, such as the PSEi. [66]

Over long periods, index funds have consistently beaten their peers. The reason is simple: index funds don't require a team of research analysts to make their decisions. Likewise, computers don't require a high salary or a large office. Instead, they can do most of the work for themselves.

One other not-so-inconsistency of index funds is holding onto their positions when the market is down. This is especially true for funds that charge high fees.

Index funds are often considered boring. On the other hand, owning a low-cost index fund while not worried about the market's performance could be a better alternative to actively managed mutual funds.

Exchange-traded and index funds are more advantageous than traditional mutual funds for investors wanting to beat the market. The Vanguard Group is the world's largest mutual-fund firm.

## Picking the Best Funds

When going camping in the wilderness, many things can help you get the most out of your experience. Some of these include planning ahead, having a GPS, and having the proper equipment and supplies.

---

[66] **An Index Fund** is a type of mutual fund or exchange-traded fund (ETF) with a portfolio constructed to match or track the components of a financial market index like the PSEi, S&P 500, etc. It's objective is to achieve the same return as a particular market index by buying and holding all or a representative selection of securities in it. (Kapoor et. Al, 2019. Personal Finance: An active Approach to Help you Achieve Financial Literacy, McGraw Hill Education, pg. 430); (Garman & Forgue, 2018. Personal Finance, Thirteenth Edition, Cengage Learning, pg. 471); (https://www.investopedia.com/terms/i/indexfund.asp)

Regardless of how much preparation time you have, there are times when you may have a hard time dealing with the things that happen in camp.

You can do it all by following these simple guidelines:

## Read Catalogs and Yearly Reports

Fund companies publish their documents in a form that investors can use to make informed decisions about their investments. For example, the most valuable information about a fund is included in its prospectus.

A good fund prospectus is typically filled with legal details, mainly composed of numbers and letters. However, instead of just focusing on the details, it also highlights the key points.

Annual reports are often the source of information that a fund needs to know about its operations. For instance, you want to know which countries a fund invests in.

## Be Low Costs

The charges that you pay for a fund can impact how much return you will get from it. Unfortunately, most novice investors make the same mistake, focusing too much on a fund's past performance and current yield. Fund fees are a part of the return that you get from a fund.

Many people are struggling with high-interest debts or underfunding their retirement plans. But, most salespeople do not provide advice on how to improve their financial situation. Instead, they often sell products that are too risky to take advantage of.

Invest in no-load (commission-free) funds. Before investing in no-load funds, check the fund's prospectus to see if it really is no-load. It is also important to avoid misleading sales and marketing hype.

## Reduce Operating Expenses

Ongoing fees are charged by funds for the various operational expenses that a fund incurs. These expenses include salaries, marketing expenses, website development, printing and mailing expenses, etc.

Operating expenses are typically quoted as a percentage of your investment. They are typically deducted each day and are invisible to the investor. Find out more about these fees by reading the fund's prospectus.

Within a particular type of fund, having low annual operating fees can increase total returns. Although expenses are typically the sole reason why funds underperform, some funds are more sensitive to them than others.

Although expenses are typically less important than expected returns, they are still significant factors that affect a fund's performance. For example, operating expenses are typically *One percent* (1%) or more than the expected returns for stock funds.

Some people believe that investing in funds that charge high expenses is justified to generate higher returns. However, this argument doesn't explain why these funds have lower rates of return.

Don't payloads and stick with funds that maintain low operating expenses. These types of fees are usually not associated with the best funds.

## Evaluate Momentous Performance

A fund's historical performance is often a vital factor to consider when selecting a fund. It shows how well the chosen fund performed in the past.

Many former high-risk funds achieved their success by taking on more risks. Since these funds tend to decline faster during market declines, they are typically considered the best funds if they deliver a favorable rate of return.

When assessing a fund's performance, compare its volatility and performance to a relevant market index over an extended period.

A stock index is a type of index that tracks the performance of a particular kind of security. Thus, it can be used to assess the performance of various kinds of stocks. [67]

## Get to Know your Fund Manager

Much of the media attention that goes to mutual fund managers are focused on who they manage.

Although the fund manager is one of the most critical factors, the capabilities and resources of a parent company are also necessary. For instance, different funds and strategies can be compared to each other based on their performance history.

Be aware that many star fund managers leave or get hired away after years of high performance, so be very careful when selecting a new manager. You must know him, look at his performance, losses, winnings, and importantly, attitude and vision.

## Identify Your Needs and Goals

You can only calculate your return by investing in more shares of the fund. Therefore, its distributions and capital gains are the ones that will give you the most return.

You have already decided what you want and need to accomplish in life. Now, it's time to determine how you're going to get there.

---

[67] An **Index** measures the price performance of a basket of securities using a standardized metric and methodology. (https://www.investopedia.com/terms/i/index.asp)

## Decoding Your Fund's Performance

A fund's share price can't be computed as it relates to the distributions it makes. So instead, it's the distribution that gives you more shares.

Even if you don't want to reinvest distributions, they can still create an accounting problem. Since they reduce the share price, they dilute the amount of money you make from the distribution.

Basically, to know how much you made or lost on your investments, compare the total value of all of your assets today with the amount you originally invested. Suppose you have invested multiple times in a row and want to factor in the timing of those investments. In that case, this exercise can be very challenging.

A fund's total return is the percentage change in its assets over a specified period. It shows how much money you invested in the fund during that period.

These three components make up your total return on a fund:

- Dividends
- Capital gains distributions
- Share price changes

In short, you calculate a fund's total return as follows:

**Dividends**
**+Capital Gains Distributions**
**+Share Price Changes**
**Total Return**

## Dividends

A fund's payouts are usually higher than the interest that the fund pays on its investment. Both stocks and bonds can also pay dividends. When a fund distributes cash or shares payment, it can be as cash or shares in the fund. The share price of the fund will then go down to offset the distribution.

Suppose you own stocks and mutual funds outside a retirement account. In that case, the distributions are taxable as long as they are received from the fund. Generally, investors are taxed at a low rate regardless of their tax bracket.

## Capital Gains

Fund managers typically sell stocks and realize a capital gain when the sale price exceeds the purchase price. This is usually a recurring annual distribution.

You can receive the capital-gains distribution as a cash distribution or as more shares in the Fund.

Suppose you own shares in a non-retirement fund that are held outside of your retirement accounts. In that case, the capital-gains distribution is subject to taxation. Long-term gains are taxed at a lower long-term rate than short-term gains.

If you're thinking about making a capital-gains distribution on investment, check with the fund to see when it will happen. This avoids generating a current-year tax liability.

## Share Price Changes

You can also make money with a fund if its share price rises. This is similar to investing in real estate, stocks, and currencies.

## Appraising and Selling Your Funds

How closely you follow your funds can vary depending on your comfort level and lifestyle. I don't recommend daily tracking the share prices of any of your investments. It can be very nerve-racking and time-consuming.

Ideally, you should not track the share prices of your funds daily. It's not necessary, as it can make you lose sight of the bigger picture.

Regular check-in is recommended to keep track of your funds. It can help you determine the exact return you're earning.

The idea that you can time and trade the markets to buy and sell at lows and highs is silly and not true.

Before selling a fund, consider selling it if it no longer meets the requirements mentioned in this section. Conversely, it can be a good time to buy funds to outperform their peers or jack up their management fees.

Looking for good funds and investing in them isn't rocket science and requires much understanding and research. Some of these include selecting suitable funds and implementing the appropriate strategies.

# Chapter 8
# Insurance: Protect What You Have

---

*The lone person who can take care of your old*
*self is the young person you are now.*
*– K.D. Tuazon*

---

Insurance is typically the most misunderstood area of personal finance. Most people would rather spend their money on something else.

Life is uncertain, and it can be dealt with through various techniques. However, because you don't want to deal with the hassles of paying for insurance when you need it most, you must look around for the best deal.

Take note that having insurance is not like having an investment.[68] But nowadays, there are flexible insurance policies already like VUL and others.[69] Investment terms are attached to them.

Here are some of the most basic insurance concepts where you can save money. While they may seem simple, they can actually save you a considerable amount.

---

[68] **Insurance** is a contract, represented by a policy, in which an individual or entity receives financial protection or reimbursement against losses from an insurance company. (Garman & Forgue, 2018. Personal Finance, Thirteenth Edition, Cengage Learning, pg. 302); (https://www. investopedia.com/terms/i/insurance.asp)

[69] **Variable Universal Life (VUL) insurance** is a type of permanent life insurance policy with a built-in savings component that allows for the investment of the cash value. It allows you to choose the investments made with your cash-value accumulations. (Garman & Forgue, 2018. Personal Finance, Thirteenth Edition, Cengage Learning, pg. 372); (https://www.investopedia. com/terms/v/variableuniversallife.asp)

## The Three Rules of Buying Insurance

### I. Insure the Big Things

What if you are having dinner at a restaurant and got food poisoning? Usually, people decline food poisoning insurance because they don't have much money at stake, especially if there is a lesser tendency to happen. It is as if you are just giving away your money.

The purpose of insurance is to protect against catastrophic losses that would have a financial impact on you. Unfortunately, some people make the same mistake many times over.

In the following sections, I will walk you through some of the most common insurance coverages available to you. I will likewise go through some of the less expensive options that are also worth your money.

### Insurance Covers Financial Catastrophes

You want to protect your family from a financial loss that could be devastating. For example, if your house was destroyed by fire, you probably would not be able to pay the bills. Fortunately, having insurance can help minimize the financial burden of rebuilding.

Think about what your most valuable assets are. Also, consider potential large expenses. Perhaps they include the following:

- **Future income:** If you were disabled during your working years, what would you live for? A long-term disability insurance policy can help you plan for the future. For example, suppose you have a family that's financially dependent on you. In that case, Life insurance can help fill the financial void left behind if you pass out.
- **Business:** When you have a business, you probably have insurance policies to protect you from negligence lawsuits. Liability insurance can protect you.
- **Health:** With healthcare costs so high these days, many people think they're healthy and then suddenly realize that

they might end up with a *One Hundred Thousand* (₱100,000) hospital bill. Major medical health insurance can help pay for many of the expenses associated with running a small business. Unfortunately, many people don't carry it anyway.

Psychologically, buying insurance for the little things that are most likely to happen is appealing. You want to feel like you're getting back some of your money because you don't want to waste it.

Suppose you were disabled and is incapable to do work or get sued for *One Million* (₱1,000,000). You may end up financially ruined. Your being upset is certain, and we do not know what might happen tomorrow.

Your insurance company uses sophisticated math to predict the likelihood of making a claim. They use this information to set their prices. They then use their actuaries to predict future claims and price their policies accordingly.

It's foolish to think that buying insurance based on your perceived likelihood of needing it is a smart idea. In fact, it can be dangerous for you to do so.

For example, two people: How much will it cost a 20-year-old for auto insurance if he lives in a high-crime area and drives a turbo sports car? And a 40-year-old, living in a low-crime area, driving a four-door sedan, and have a clean driving record?

## Get the Highest Deductible You Can Manage

Most insurance policies have a deductible. The amount you pay when your insurance coverage begins to payout is usually the maximum amount you can afford before the coverage kicks in.

Here are some benefits of taking a higher deductible:

- **You save premium.** Year in and year out, you can save money on your insurance policy by increasing your deductible. For instance, by raising your deductible to *Fifty Thousand* (₱50,000), you can reduce your annual cost by *Seven Thousand Five undred* (₱7,500).

- **Hassle-free of filing small claims.** Having a small claim is a lot easier than filing a large one. For instance, if you have a loss on a policy with a *Ten Thousand* (₱10,000) deductible, you must submit a claim to get the *Ten Thousand* (₱10,000). However, doing so can be an arduous process.

You may also file more claims if you have low deductibles. However, this may mean that you will not get more money, resulting in higher premiums.

## Avoid Small-scale Policies

A good policy can seem expensive. However, suppose you are not sure about the amount of coverage you're getting. In that case, a policy that doesn't cost much can be very misleading.

Below are some examples of common small-scale insurance policies that are usually worthless. Unfortunately, they may feel like they were paid for themselves.

- **Extended warranty and repair plans.** It is ironic that after a salesman or company convinces you to buy a particular product, they try further to convince you to spend more on extended warranties and repair plans. Many consumers are unaware that there are often hidden costs associated with extended warranties and repair plans. Most of the time, these policies are only available for a limited amount of time. Therefore, they are not worth the money if they ever happen.
- **Home warranty plans.** If you're planning about selling a house, you might want to consider a house warranty plan instead of paying the agent or seller the plan's cost. While it seems to be a great deal, consider the plan's terms and conditions. Your money is best spent on hiring a competent inspector to find issues before buying a house.

- **Dental insurance.** If you're offered dental insurance, you can take it up. Just make sure that you pay for it on your own instead of relying on it.
- **Credit life and credit disability policies.** If you die without a loan, credit life policies can provide a small benefit to pay off your debts. If you have a credit card, a credit disability policy can help pay off your debts. Although the cost may seem low, it has little to no potential benefits. So instead of buying it, get enough coverage and pay for it in a separate policy. If you have poor health and can buy insurance policies, you may be an exception to the rule. This is because these policies are usually the only ones that can be used by people with poor health.
- **Daily hospitalization insurance.** Daily hospitalization policies are typically sold to people worried about running up large hospital bills. A comprehensive health insurance policy is the type of policy that will cover the major expenses of a hospital stay. Usually, a hospital stay costs thousands of pesos, and many of these expenses are covered by a policy.
- **Cellphone insurance.** However, I understand that if you paid for a new smartphone and it gets damaged or lost, you might want to protect yourself against this expense. However, I also think that if you insist on having the insurance, it will cost you a huge sum of money.
- **Small stuff add-ons.** Some policies that are worth buying have extras that can be added on. These riders are often added on to make them more profitable for insurance companies and agents. One example is a rider that pays you whenever your car is towed.

Similarly, buying small insurance is also not an unnecessary add-on to a more comprehensive policy. For example, if you need life insurance, you can get it in a separate policy.

## II. *Get a Comprehensive Coverage*

People tend to mistake purchasing policies that are too narrow to cover all of their needs. For instance, some people tend to buy flight insurance for their travel accommodations at an airport.

They seem to be more anxious about their mortality when they get on an airplane than when they get into a car.

Life insurance is a type of insurance that can protect your loved ones in the event of your untimely death.

A cancer insurance policy is like flight insurance. It only pays for cancer treatment and doesn't cover other major medical expenses. If you get cancer, your insurance won't pay for the treatments and procedures that you need. So instead, you should buy a medical insurance policy.

Not being well protected from certain risks is a simple reason why many people buy insurance. But, there are particular ways to reduce your exposure to these risks and still be well protected.

You can't buy a policy that prevents drunk drivers from getting behind the wheel. But, you can consider some things to minimize risks while driving.

## *Prepare for Natural Disasters*

In the following chapters, various types of insurances were discussed, such as homeowner's and disability insurance, which are almost impossible to get coverage for if you live in areas with certain risks.

When you buy a house insurance policy, many of the coverages exclude losses from earthquakes and floods. This is because most insurers don't always explain these risks to their customers.

Aside from filling the voids, also think about the non-financial issues that arise when a disaster strikes.

- A dwelling to meet with family and friends if you're separated during a disaster.
- Having a disaster escape plan is vital when dealing with natural disasters such as earthquakes, storms, floods, etc. It can help you get out of the way when dealing with the aftermath of any

catastrophic event. A plan for what you'll do if your home gets destroyed.

Even though it can't predict what will happen, you can still get a handle on the risks involved in your area. In addition, having a plan in place can help you prepare for emergencies.

## III. Compare Before you Buy

Some companies charge double or triple the rates they charge for the same coverage. This means that they may be better at paying claims than the other companies.

Most insurance is sold through intermediaries, who earn commissions based on the amount they sell.

The bigger the commissions that insurance companies offer, the more expensive the policies are. This is because the bigger the commissions, the more agents are likely to sell the insurance policies.

Not only are agents incentivized to sell more insurance policies, but they also get rich doing it.

Because most insurance companies are not selling commissions, finding the best deal can be a challenge. Insurers also set their rates in mysterious ways, which can affect how much risk you take.

Despite the obstacles, there are still ways to get high-quality policies at low prices.

### Getting Insurance Without Reimbursing Sales Commissions

Since many companies are now selling insurance policies directly to the public, it is always good to shop around for a better price. Just as with no-load mutual funds, you can also buy no-load insurance from an investment company. Again, this can be done without paying any sales commission.

Annuities, typically sold through insurance agents, can now be offered without commission through no-load mutual funds.

## Protect Your Loved Ones: Life Insurance

You generally don't need life insurance to protect your income if other people depend on it.

- Single people with no children
- Working couples maintaining an acceptable lifestyle
- Wealthy people who are independent
- Retired people who are dependent on their pension
- Minor children

If others are dependent on your paycheck, life insurance is a good idea. Then, you will be protected from financial hardship if you suddenly become unable to work.

### Identify Your Life Insurance Coverage

The amount of life insurance that you need is as subjective as it is quantitative. There are many ways to determine how much insurance to buy. Unfortunately, doing so can be very long and complex.

Life insurance is a form of payment that provides a lump sum to replace the deceased person's income.[70] To determine how much insurance to purchase, you should ask yourself how many years you want to replace.

One way to determine the amount of life insurance you should buy is by taking the debts you need to pay for your children's college education and mortgage.

---

[70] **A life insurance policy** is a contract between an insured (the policy holder) and the insurer. It guarantees the insurer pays a sum of money to named beneficiaries when the insured dies in exchange for the premiums paid by the policyholder during their lifetime. (Garman & Forgue, 2018. Personal Finance, Thirteenth Edition, Cengage Learning, pg. 373); (https://www. investopedia.com/terms/l/lifeinsurance.asp)

**The DIME method**[71]

Calculations depend on your Insurance company. If you want to look at the entire picture of your coverage, you can use the DIME method. Debt, Income, Mortgage, and Education. In this method, you record up the following to conclude the extent of coverage you can have:

- Unsettled debts
- Total earnings multiplied by the number of years your family will depend on it
- The amount left on your mortgage
- The cost of your children's education

Sum total of all these factors shall be the coverage of life insurance you should buy.

---

[71] https://www.policygenius.com/life-insurance/how-much-life-insurance-do-i-need/

# Chapter 9
# Blueprint for Financial Success

---

*Financial security and independence are like a three-legged stool resting on savings, insurance, and investments.*
*– Brian Tracy*

---

Some life changes are predictable, while others can be unexpected. Some of these are natural disasters, like earthquakes. Others can be triggered by events that happen far beyond our expectations.

Here are some common tips that apply to all types of life changes:

- **Stay financially fit.** Being in good financial condition will help you endure the challenges of competing in an athletic environment. Having a healthy and balanced diet will also help you avoid experiencing weight gain and other health issues.
- **Changes require change.** Change is inevitable. Though you are in good financial shape, a significant life change may require reassessing your financial strategies. It might also affect your ability to manage risk. Be adaptable to changes.
- **Don't procrastinate.** Don't postpone things most especially if they will contribute to your goals and dreams. Act immediately. Having a significant life change can be costly. It can also lead to unforeseen expenses. Not planning for a meaningful life change can be very expensive. In addition, it can create issues, such as not having the proper insurance coverage or managing your debts.
- **Manage stress and your emotions.** When dealing with stress and other emotional upheavals, don't make snap decisions. Instead, learn to manage your emotions and become fully aware of them. Proper advisors can help you make informed decisions, but they may not be in your best interests. Don't decide when you are emotional. It will bring you in the wrong direction.

Here are the significant changes you may have to face in your life. I wish you more strength and good changes.

## Getting Started

It is good to have graduated from college or even entered the workforce. However, many young adults still face financial difficulties due to their lack of discipline and poor habits.

Consider the following to get on the path to financial success:

- **Use consumer credit wisely.** The use of credit cards can cause long-term financial problems if mismanaged. Young workers should avoid carrying credit cards and make purchases with debit cards instead. Doing so will help them get off on the right financial footing.
- **Master the skills in saving and investing.** Saving and investing will give you the desired amount of money you need to accumulate in your retirement accounts that offer tax advantages. I am often asked, *What is the desired age to save and invest?* I like to answer, *Well, when I have teeth to brush, I should start doing so.* The earlier, the better. Now is the time to start saving!
- **Get insured.** Young people tend to underestimate the financial impact of unforeseen expenses. Whether it is due to an accident or a long-term illness, getting insurance can help minimize the financial burden of these unexpected events. When you start a new job, it pays to consider buying disability insurance. It can replace the income that you lost due to a disability, and it can also help preserve your assets.
- **Continue your education.** After you get out of school, think about how much you learned in school that can be used in the real world. After you have worked, you realize that you didn't get enough in school. School may not always be the best option for everyone, especially those who can't afford it. But if there's a chance, grab it. Your learning should be continuous. The good thing is that, you can learn from your experiences and the experiences of others. Find mentors you can lean on. Read their

books if they are authors. Learn from them. Master the skill of *unlearning* and *learning*. Unlearn the obsolete knowledge and learn new things. Be a student who is hungry of knowledge all the time.

## Finding for Your Passion/Career

During your adult life, you will probably change jobs. It's not uncommon for people to do so several times a decade. Even with the steady decline in job security, many people still believe that they have job security. This is not true.

Being prepared for a job change can help you feel more secure and at peace with the world. Having this idea can also help prepare for the unexpected.

- **Organize your finances to afford an income fluctuation.** Structure your finances to avoid a short-term income dip. It is important to set aside a portion of your income to pay off debts and maintain a budget for emergencies. Many people see thriftiness as restrictive, but it gives them more freedom to do what they want. In addition, having an emergency reserve fund can help ensure that they have enough funds to pay for unexpected expenses.

You have to review your current spending patterns to ensure that they're not going to drag you down. This will help avoid making the same mistakes that cost you and your goals in the first place.

- **Evaluate the total financial picture when relocating.** Before you decide to move, take time to analyze the financial picture of the move. It is important to understand the various aspects of your action, such as income, salaries, benefits, and the cost of living.

## Settling for Marriage

If you're not yet ready to tie the knot, there are a few things you should prepare-for once you are married. Even if the spouses have agreed on many of the goals and strategies related to financial management, managing two is different from managing as one.

Here's how to prepare:

- **Discuss and set joint goals.** After getting married, start setting aside time to discuss and set mutual goals. This will help ensure that both of you are on the same financial path going forward.
- **Make a decision to keep finances separate or jointly managed.** Whether to keep your money separate or manage it jointly is a decision that will affect both of you. To avoid financial quarrels during your marriage, be transparent, don't hide money, transactions, or debts.
- **Discuss life and disability insurance needs.** For example, suppose you and your spouse can no longer make do without each other's income. In that case, you may not need income-protecting insurance. On the other hand, if you both depend on each other's income, you may need long-term disability and life insurance policies.
- **Update your wills.** You have to update your will when you marry. Having a will makes it much easier to leave your money and properties to your heirs. It also helps to name a guardian for them.
- **Reconsider beneficiaries on investment and life insurance.** The beneficiaries of your life and retirement accounts should be noted. Having the right people on board can help ensure that your money will be used after you pass away.

## Having a Home

Most people eventually buy a house. Owning one doesn't mean you are successful, but homeownership can be very rewarding. Be sure first that you have sources of income before having one. If you're thinking about buying a house, take these steps:

- **Get your overall finances in order.** Have a look at your current financial situation and goals before buying a house. This will help you make informed decisions about how to save and afford a house.
- **Determine whether now's the time.** If you don't see yourself settling for a long time, buying a house may be the wrong choice. However, if you have other financial goals, then wait to buy.

## Having Children

While it's hard to imagine being a responsible adult, having kids can be even more challenging. Most parents find it hard to manage their time and money when they have children. The sooner you learn how to do this, the better off you will be. These are the things to do before and after you begin your family:

- **Fix your priorities.** Starting a family can be a challenging financial decision, but it can be done ahead of time. By choosing your priorities, you can structure your financial situation in a way that works for you. A less busy work life can also reduce your cost of living.
- **Take a hard look at your budget.** Before you start planning for your kids' future, take a look at your current budget. It will tell you how much you should spend on various expenses. If you plan to be a full-time parent, working may not be an option. This is because working at a full-time job usually requires a reduction in income.

How do you want to cut back expenses, and how much do you want to raise kids? A more scientific approach to estimating how much kids will change your budget is used.

- **Boost insurance coverage before getting pregnant.** Before having a baby, make sure that you have health insurance in place. Even if you don't have coverage, you can still enroll during the open enrollment period. Having disability insurance is also a good idea for women who are expecting. It is also a good idea to secure life insurance before the baby is born. However, buying life insurance after the child is born can be risky. Enroll the baby in your health plan. After you welcome the baby, enroll him in the insurance plan that's right for you. Most insurance companies give you a month to register.
- **Don't indulge the children.** Don't spend extravagantly on the children. Even if you have the money to spend, don't indulge them. Unfortunately, other parents follow the example of their peers. Most parents I know have experienced the same anxiety and fear about raising their kids. The only difference is that they seem to be the most financially successful.

As kids get older, they may realize that they can also buy other things for themselves. Having a weekly allowance can help teach them how to manage their money.

## *Opening a Small Business*

Most people aspire to be their own boss, but many of them actually leave their jobs for that dream to become a reality. Getting started is not for everyone, and it can be challenging if you don't believe in yourself. Consider these tips to get started and increase your chances for long-term success:

- **Prepare to burn your bridge.** While preparing to leave your job, prepare to live a Spartan lifestyle. It will help you manage the increased expenses and minimize the stress of starting a small business.
- **Envision the destination of your business.** Your vision for your business will determine its future. Clear your mind on the direction of your business and focus on going there. The journey will be a curvy road. Endure it and hold the vision. You must trust the process. If you can visualize the success of

your business, no matter what comes your way, you will never give up.

- **Develop a business plan.** A good business plan helps you develop an action plan that outlines all the details of your venture. It can also help minimize the risk of failing. A good business plan shows how you plan on operating and growing your company. It describes in detail your strategies for profitability, sales, and expenses.
- **Keep your burning desire.** Building a business is a tough challenge. It may seem straightforward if you have enough skills and resources. Still, the business cycle will test your faith and persistency. Most businesses fail not because of any reason but it is because the owner quit pursuing its vision. Great author Napoleon Hill quoted, *Every person who wins in any undertaking must be willing to cut all sources of retreat. Only by doing so can one be sure of maintaining that state of mind known as a burning desire to win - essential to success.*[72] Always remember that your ultimate victory will often come just one step beyond the point at which defeat has overtaken you.

## Retiring

If you spent most of your adult life working, then you might be thinking about retiring. But, as with most people, you might not plan ahead. So here are some tips to help you through retirement:

- **Plan both financially and personally.** Planning for the future can be as important as planning for the present. If you only focus on saving money, you may not have the time to prepare for the future. Plan well how you can invest your money to make it work for you while achieving your goals.

---

[72] **Napoleon Hill**, a famous American author and big influencer on the key to success and personal achievement. Most people know him from the 17 Principles of Success and his best sellers the law of success and Think and Grow Rich, which sold more than 20 million copies. He discovered a secret, described as "the Golden Rule." It is only by working harmoniously in co-operation with other individuals or groups of individuals and thus creating value and benefit for them will one create sustainable achievement for oneself.

- **Consolidate all your resources.** Many people worry about their financial security and wonder if they have enough assets to retire or cut back from work. However, this often leads to people assuming that their assets are too little or too much. So it's better to have visuals on your assets to know if you have enough.
- **Reevaluate your insurance needs.** When you have enough assets to retire, it is time to evaluate your insurance needs. On the other hand, if your assets grow over the years and you become underinsured. It may be time to consider additional investment vehicles fitted to your risk tolerance.
- **Evaluate healthcare/living options.** Living expenses for your retirement years can be challenging. However, there are many options for addressing these expenses, like building a business or investing in financial securities.
- **Choose where to put your retirement money.** If you have retirement savings, it's your choice to roll it over into your own account. However, it can also give you more options and better investment returns.
- **Get your estate in order.** Estate planning is a smart way to prepare for retirement. It can help avoid surprises when it comes to planning for your future. There are a variety of wills and trusts that can benefit both you and your heirs.

# Book References

**Napoleon Hill,** *Think and Grow Rich*
**Rhonda Byrne,** *The Secret*
**John C. Maxwell,** *How Successful People Think*
**John C. Maxwell,** *The Success Journey*
**T. Harv Eker,** *Secrets to a Millionaire Mind*
**Robert Kiyosaki,** *Rich Dad, Poor Dad*
**Robert Kiyosaki,** *Rich Dad's Cashflow Quadrant*
**Robert Kiyosaki,** *Increase your Financial IQ*
**Jim Rohn,** *The Art of Exceptional Living*
**Steven Covey,** *Seven Habits of Highly Successful People*
**Chinkee Tan,** *Secrets of the Rich and Successful*
**Chinkee Tan,** *Till Debt do us Part*
**Bo Sanchez,** *8 Secrets of the Truly Rich*
**Randell Tiongson,** *No Nonsense Personal Finance*
**Marvin Germo,** *Stock Investing Made easy*
**George Samuel Clason,** *The Richest Man in Babylon*
**Joel Lerner,** *Financial Planning for the Utterly Confused*
**Brent Donnelly,** *The Art of Currency Trading*

## Textbooks:

**Kapoor et al., 2019.** *Personal Finance: An Active Approach to Help You Achieve Financial Literacy, McGraw Hill Education*

**Garman & Forgue, 2018.** *Personal Finance, Thirteenth Edition, Cengage Learning*

## Online References:

https://www.investopedia.com
https://www.pesolab.com

# Tips for Financial Success

- **Your finances, your responsibility.** Sometimes we are good at postponements and delays. Procrastination is harmful to your financial health. Don't wait for a specific financial problem or economic crisis to push your action. Understand this book and learn how to regain and maintain your financial health!
- **Show off now, be broke later.** Don't live beyond your means, and don't try to compete with your co-workers, neighbors, and friends. Most of those who engage in obvious consumption are borrowing against their future; some end up broke.
- **Misusing credit cards will compromise your net worth.** Credit cards are good, but use them only to purchase your needs like food, not high debt. If you tend to not control yourself and run into credit card debt, keep your cards and use only cash, checks, and debit cards.
- **Save and Invest now; play later.** Save and invest at least *Thirty percent to Fifty percent* (30% - 50%) of your income. Preferably, invest through a profitable portfolio, investment vehicle, or trusted broker to reduce your taxes and ensure your future financial independence.
- **Be employed to learn and master a skill.** Understand and use your employee benefits to grow mentally and financially. Being self-employed is good, but find the best investment and insurance options available to you and use them.
- **Avoid deceptive and impulsive buying.** Think and research before you purchase. Never buy a financial product or service based on an advertisement or salesperson's solicitation and opinion. If you want something, wait for *Thirty* (30) days, this will help you confirm if you really need the product or service.
- **Scrutinize and compare before you buy.** Avoid purchasing without comparing and canvassing. Comparing the items to buy will save you money and avoid costly purchases.
- **Learn before you earn or learn while you earn.** Only purchase financial products that you know and comprehend. If you don't know about it yet, make time to study it. To learn something

means you are growing. Earning requires learning. If you are new to a specific venture or investment, know the basics. Sooner or later, you will become an expert at them, be a consistent learner.

- **Think of the temporary but always focus on the permanent.** Invest most of your money or savings in investment vehicles with growth potentials, such as stocks, real estate, and your own business. It's good to think short-term, but considering the long-term will give you a sense of stability. Investing in bonds or in banks accounts means that you lent your funds to others. The effect is that the return you earn probably won't keep you ahead of inflation and taxes.
- **Don't be too emotional.** If you can control your emotions, you are in control of everything. Don't make emotionally centered financial decisions. For instance, an investor with fear and selling his stock position after a significant market correction misses a buying opportunity. Be careful in making important financial decisions after a significant life change, such as a job loss or bankruptcy.
- **Get protected and be insured.** Eliminate insurance for small potential losses. Protect yourself, your family, and your assets. It's better to be prepared and ready.
- **Read. Read. Read.** Financial books and articles are your battle tools against financial inconsistencies and financial problems. First, read publications with quality standards to guide you towards your financial journey and recommend what's in your best interests. Then, apply what you have read. Avoid articles that based their content on the hottest financial headlines.
- **Highlight your financial target and work smart.** Make your financial goals your priority, and start working on them now. Consider patience. Focus on your undertakings and learn from your shortcomings.
- **Trust yourself.** Treat yourself as your first priority. You are your best critique, but don't let yourself down, instead, trust yourself. In making a significant financial decision, communicate with conflict-free consultants who charge nothing for their time to help you out. Work in trust with mentors and filter the learning that could benefit you in your financial health.

- **Invest in yourself and others.** You are your own great weapon. Invest in your learning, your health, and your relationships with your family and friends. Being rich in money isn't worth much if you don't have your health and people to share your life with. Give your time and money to things that better our society and world.

# Author's Acknowledgement

Thank you, Father Almighty, for the gift of wisdom!

Being an entrepreneur requires a lot of support and encouragement from people close to me. This is why I'm so grateful for the support and assistance I had received from them.

I hold many people responsible for my creative fascination with money matters and the financial services industry. However, most of the blame falls on my parents. They taught me what I know about the real world.

I am humbled to acknowledge my mentors for their support and for helping me with my writing most specially to my uncle Danilo Duque.

To all the people who believed and challenged me, thank you so much!

# About the Author

A Teacher, Entrepreneur, Stock Trader, and a Value Investor.

He received his Bachelor's degree in Business Administration major in Financial Management from the University of Saint Louis Tuguegarao, Philippines. He is currently teaching Business and Finance courses at the same university and strongly advocates financial literacy and financial management. His professional interests focused on Personal Financial Management and Financial Researches, and his current projects include book publications in the field of Business and Finance. In addition, he is a member of the Philippine Council of Deans And Educators In Business (PCDEB) and the Association of Marketing Educators of the Philippines, Inc (AME). He also took his Doctor of Laws at the University of Cagayan Valley and is earning his Masters Degree in Business Administration at the same university.

At a young age, he had already started trading and investing in the stock market. After mastering the necessary skills, he started trading in the Forex and International Stock Market. While doing other side hustles, he also devoted his time to expanding his marketing and business management knowledge.

Printed in the United States
by Baker & Taylor Publisher Services